MW01118161

A Short History of Income Tax in America

1861 - Congress passes Revenue Act ordering a tax on personal income to pay for Civil War.

1871 – Revenue Act taxes repealed ten years later.

1894 - Congress enacts flat rate Federal income tax against wealthiest citizens.

1895 – U.S. Supreme Court declares 1894 Federal income tax unconstitutional.

1913 – Congress overrules Supreme Court by passing 16th Amendment allowing government to tax all personal and business income.

1918 – Federal income taxes collected for 1917 more than 1 billion dollars.

1920 – Federal income tax transfers $5.4 billion from people to government.

1945 – Congress grabs $43 billion in income through Federal income tax program.

2007 – Federal government nets $2.4 trillion in taxes, after all refunds issued.

ANNUAL TAX MESS ORGANIZER

FOR

SALES CONSULTANTS

& HOME PARTY SALES REPS

(2nd Edition)

By

KiKi Canniff

ANNUAL TAX MESS ORGANIZER

FOR

SALES CONSULTANTS

& HOME PARTY SALES REPS

Published by
ONE MORE PRESS
www.OneMorePress.com

Legal Disclaimer

The information in this book was published for the purpose of providing tax education to U.S. taxpayers and small business owners, and not for providing accounting or legal advice. The author does not make express or implied warranties in regard to the use of the enclosed information.

Cover Design

Heather Kibbey - Northwest Publishers Consortium - Lake Oswego, OR - www.NPCBooks.com

ISBN: 978-0-941361453

Dedication

This book is dedicated to self-employed sales representatives all across America. Knowing that many of you don't file taxes at all, because the rules are too confusing, and that most independent contractors who do file taxes annually pay more tax than the law requires, I wrote this book for you.

Acknowledgment

It is with great appreciation that I acknowledge the Internal Revenue Service and those elected officials and federal employees who write our tax laws and tax instruction manuals. For without the confusion created by these dedicated government employees there would be no need for this book.

TABLE OF CONTENTS

ANNUAL TAX MESS ORGANIZER

FOR

SALES CONSULTANTS

& HOME PARTY SALES REPS

HOW THIS ORGANIZER WORKS

This Annual Tax Mess Organizer is for home party planners and independent sales consultants who have not kept itemized income and expense records as the year went along. For some of you it's your first business tax season; others have run their business this way for years. You might be hosting parties and selling scrapbooking supplies, plastic storage containers, weight loss products, vitamins, makeup, adult items, frozen food plans, or one of the many other products sold door to door and/or thru home parties.

Now that April 15th is getting close, you're stressed out, and forced to put your new sales efforts on hold while you deal with a disorganized pile of receipts and paperwork that sits between you and that quickly approaching tax deadline.

This organizer will show you how to whip that pile of paperwork into order fast, so you can satisfy the IRS and get back to work. It teaches you a simple, once-a-year method for organizing small business records, and explains what the IRS expects of a self-employed business person.

The examples cover a variety of situations, in an attempt to provide examples that can be applied to all types of self-employment situations.

Step by step, the Annual Tax Mess Organizer walks you through the sorting process helping you to get everything organized and ready for your tax preparer.

For those who have always done their own personal tax return, there is a chapter on how to fill out a Schedule C, the small business tax form. It walks you through the form, line by line, telling you where to post all of the information you've gathered.

If you have not done your own taxes in the past skip the section on posting the information to your tax return and instead, take the numbers you have gathered to a licensed professional tax preparer.

This book does not teach you how to do your own taxes; the chapter on filling out your Schedule C tax form merely shows you where to post the information you have gathered.

If you have deposited all of your business income into just one bank account, and kept all of your expense receipts together, this organizer will have you ready for the tax preparer in 1-3 hours.

Even if your records are a total mess, you should be done in less than 4 hours, once you've located all of the necessary paperwork.

The final chapter in this book explains how easy it is to win a tax audit.

What You Need

Basic math is the only skill you need to get your business records ready for the tax professional.

You will also need the following:

- One spiral notebook containing lined paper
- 25 large envelopes
- Adding machine
- Empty table or desktop

The envelopes can be 6x9 if you don't have many receipts, bigger if your business generates lots of paperwork. If you don't have large envelopes on hand, and your pile of paperwork is small, you can substitute 25 sheets of paper for the envelopes.

If you buy an adding machine with a paper tape you'll make fewer mistakes. Running a paper tape twice is a terrific way to check your math; when the numbers don't match you've entered something wrong. Add them again until you get two matching numbers.

The organization process is fairly simple, once you've learned how. And, you'll find tips for making the process faster next year.

GETTING DOWN TO BUSINESS

Tracking business income is a snap, once you learn to follow Tax Pro Rule #1.

Tax Pro Rule #1

Absolutely all business income,

including all cash & tips,

must be deposited into a separate checking account

used only for business funds.

To survive an IRS audit, you need to maintain a separate checking account for your business. Otherwise, the IRS can question every deposit and expense co-mingled with your personal funds, and your tax bill may be higher than necessary.

Many banks offer free checking, and it makes no difference to the IRS whether this account is in your personal or business name. So, if you don't already have one, open a business account today, and follow Tax Pro Rule #1.

Tracking business expenses is just as easy. Look at Tax Pro Rule #2.

Tax Pro Rule #2

Every penny spent or charged for your business

needs a paper trail. If a receipt

is not provided, you can make your own,

just include all of the necessary details.

When you use your debit card or write a check you leave a paper trail, but following that trail a year later can be confusing. It's a lot easier to work from actual receipts.

Getting a receipt for every purchase is the best method, but you can make your own when a receipt is not available. When writing your own receipt you will need to note the date, how much you spent, what you purchased, and who got the money. Carry a small bound notepad in the car for little purchases; you can sort and total them at tax time. Keep an envelope there too, for stashing loose receipts.

Follow those first two Tax Pro Rules and you'll cut your tax prep time in half next year.

STEP ONE: TRACKING YOUR INCOME

If you already have a separate checking account, and you deposited all funds into that account, all you need to track your income are your 12 bank statements for the tax year.

Open up your notebook, and on the first empty page write BUSINESS INCOME across the top. Now write the amount shown as Total Monthly Deposits from each bank statement, onto your Business Income sheet. Total those deposits and you will have your total income deposited during the year.

Get a large envelope and write BUSINESS INCOME across the top. Write this total on the front of the envelope and put those bank statements inside. Business bank statements should always be stored with your business tax records.

If you do any barter, trading your goods or business services with another for goods or services, that too must be reported as income according to the IRS.

Tax Pro Rule #3

Every business barter exchange requires

a paper trail assigning value to your time,

or the product you traded

for another's time or product.

You are expected to count as income the value of every barter exchange. The value of a barter exchange is what you would have charged if that person had paid you in cash. If you trade goods or inventory during a barter exchange, those costs will be deducted along with other expenses; for now we're only concerned with barter income.

Post the total value of all barter exchanges to the front of the Business Income envelope and label it Barter Income. Write the total of all barter income on your Business Income sheet too.

If you rent an office or show space, and you collect rent from others, in exchange for part of your office or show space, you need to track this income separately.

Write the total amount collected as Rental Income on both your Business Income sheet and on the front of the Business Income envelope.

Space rent in a business where you also work is posted to your Schedule C, and not put on the IRS rental property form.

Looking for Income

If you weren't organized you're not totally out of luck; it will just take a little longer to figure out how much money you made in your business this year. Most income can be found by answering two questions.

Income Question #1: Where did you deposit the checks?

The first place to look would be your personal bank account.

Grab the checkbook register and highlight every deposit that was made with business income. Total up all of those business deposits and enter that figure on the front of the Business Income envelope as well as on the Business Income Sheet, noting the account where it was deposited.

You will need to save those checkbook registers with other business receipts, in case of an audit.

If you deposited business income into more than one personal bank account, repeat the above procedure on each account.

Because you have co-mingled funds, the burden of proof will be on you if an audit is scheduled. You will be required to prove that all other deposits in those accounts were not business income.

Paychecks will be easy, but any cash gifts or other unsubstantiated deposits will cause problems, and could be taxed as business income. The bottom line in an audit is, if you can't prove otherwise the auditor can count those deposits as income.

This is one of the biggest reasons why you want to open a business checking account, to keep the IRS out of your personal bank account.

Income Question #2: What did you do with the cash?

Cash income can be tricky.

Business income is taxed whether you receive it as a check, cash, barter, or in any other form. The government wants their share, and if the IRS comes looking, and you have no records, you could end up paying taxes you don't owe.

For most independent business people, writing all cash income on a calendar any time they are paid in cash is enough proof for the IRS.

Consistency in reporting is the key for calendar-style reporting. Someone running a retail store would need a register-style cash reporting system, the calendar method is only for those who receive occasional cash payments or tip income.

You also need to deposit ALL of your cash income into your business bank account. You can do this daily, weekly, or as needed.

If you use a calendar for tracking cash income, you must record every penny of cash income on that calendar, or it can be disqualified. The IRS rules state that when you do not account for all cash income in a consistent manner, they can decide how much cash income you made based on industry standards.

If you get audited, and you did not keep proper records, you're sunk. So make a plan to keep better records in the future, do your best to come up with the right amount this year, and cross your fingers that you're not audited.

Post the total of all income found to the front of your Business Income envelope as well as to the Business Income sheet in your notebook.

Put all paperwork, including cash calendars, into the Business Income envelope.

Computing Gross Business Income

All you have to do now is add up all bank deposits, barter values, space rent, and cash income posted to your Business Income sheet.

This total is what the IRS refers to as your Gross Business Income. It is not your taxable business income, there's more work to be done before you will know what amount will be taxed, if any.

Write TOTAL GROSS INCOME on your Business Income sheet and enter your total. Also enter this amount on the front of your Business Income envelope. You are finished with the Business Income sheet for now. Later, you will come back to this page for that Total Gross Income figure.

For now, set the Business Income envelope aside; you won't need it again. You'll learn about tax record storage in the final chapter.

STEP TWO: TRACKING YOUR EXPENSES

How fast you're done with this step depends on whether or not you're organized. If it's easy for you to get your hands on your business expense receipts, it won't take long at all.

If those receipts are all shoved into a shoe box, you're actually in luck. All you need to do is sort them, and this book teaches you how to do it quickly.

For the totally unorganized, now is the time when you're forced to search high and low for any receipt or recollection of money spent on your business. Here are some good places to look.

Start with your checkbook register, credit card records, debit statements and bank accounts; highlight all business expenses found. Now dig thru your car, coat pockets, briefcase or purse, and anywhere else you normally shove papers to see if any receipts have been left there. Look thru your personal receipts and see if any business receipts were misfiled.

If you have clients, and purchase goods to complete work for them, you may find receipts in with client records. Look around your place of business to jog your memory for equipment purchased during the tax year, and in general, do everything you can to locate receipts and reconstruct expense records.

Business expenses are generally 100% deductible from business income. But, you must know what you spent in order to take that deduction. Guessing is not allowed; without a paper trail you will fail an IRS audit.

If you want to pay less in taxes, take the time to track down every legitimate expense. The savings could easily be several hundred dollars.

Organizing Expense Receipts

Sorting expense receipts is simple, once you learn the business expense alphabet. This book includes a simple ABC sorting procedure that is quick and easy.

Tax Pro Rule #4

Sorting expense receipts

is as easy as ABC, when you use

the business expense alphabet.

To help you organize your expense receipts quickly, you're going to label the rest of those large envelopes and use them as guides to sort your expense receipts.

All totals will be written on the front of the envelopes, and eventually all receipts will be tucked inside.

Creating Expense Envelopes

Across the top of each envelope, write one of the alphabetical titles from the list below. Use a dark pen so you can see it quickly; keep it near the top of the envelope so it won't get covered by papers as you sort.

Each envelope represents a deductible classification as defined by the IRS.

A Advertising & Promotional Expenses

B Bank, Visa & Other Business Interest Paid

C Cleaning Materials & Business Supplies

D Donations to Nonprofit Organizations

E Educational Seminars & Classes

F Fix-it & Repair Expenses

G Gifts

H Home Office Expenses

I Insurance

J Job Required Licenses & Dues

L Legal & Professional Fees

M Meals & Entertainment

N Newspapers, Magazines & Subscriptions

O Office Supplies

P People Who Take a Share

Q Equipment Purchased

R Rent Paid

S Shipping & Postage

T Travel

U Utilities

V Vehicle (Car/Truck) Expenses

W Wages & Contract Labor Expenses

X Taxes & Business Licenses

Z Inventory

Now that you have all of your expense envelopes labeled, read the following information explaining which expenses belong in each category. When you're finished, you'll be ready to sort those expense receipts.

What is Deductible?

Hobby income is not considered business income, because the intent is not profit motivated. The IRS classifies hobby income as miscellaneous income. Hobby expense deductions are limited to hobby income; both are posted directly to your 1040 personal tax return.

To be considered a business you must be profit motivated. If you repeatedly post a business loss you may be asked to prove that you are actively seeking income. This is easy to prove if you have a current written business plan.

Business profit is calculated using IRS Form Schedule C, before it is posted to your 1040 personal tax return. IRS rules permit a business owner to deduct every ordinary and necessary expense incurred during the production of, or attempt to produce, legitimate income.

A small business owner may also deduct the expense involved in operating a home office, business mileage or depreciation on vehicles, and interest on business-only debts, including credit cards and home equity mortgages.

If you purchase self-employed health insurance, or make IRA or other retirement deposits, these costs are posted to your personal 1040 tax return, not your Schedule C business return.

Self-employment taxes fund your Social Security and Medicare accounts, and are also posted to your 1040 tax return.

Be sure to take all of the figures for self-employed health insurance costs and retirement fund contributions with you when you visit your tax professional.

If you are doing your own tax return, you'll need to add those expenses to your 1040, and calculate your own self-employment tax. In the chapter on preparing your own business tax return you'll learn how to calculate that tax and where those other business deductions are posted.

The more you know about what you're allowed to deduct, the quicker the sorting process will go, and the more items you will deduct with confidence. Remember, for every legitimate expense you subtract you decrease taxable income, keeping more money in your own pocket.

Read the following ABC expense category descriptions before you start to sort.

A - Advertising & Promotional Expenses

This category includes business cards, phone book ads, newspaper & magazine advertisements, flyer inserts, school sponsorships, coupon books, and all other money spent to promote or advertise your business.

If you spent money, or traded goods or an employee's services, to get your business name or product out to the public, it's deductible.

For a party sales rep, promotional expenses could include food, prizes, and decorations purchased to entice people over to your table at a free event, as well as all expenses involved in booking and promoting your product or any individual party or event you are hosting.

If you rent table or booth space at a fair, bazaar, or event, all money spent to get both yourself and your product to that event, bazaar, or fair where it can be sold, is deductible.

All one-time or reusable party or holiday decorations that you purchase for use at a particular party, plus all door prizes, gifts, food, entertainment supplies, catering service fees, treats, or other "normal" costs involved in promoting your business, are also considered advertising expenses.

Always separate all sample costs from inventory expenses; sample costs belong in with other advertising and promotional expenses.

B - Bank, Visa & Other Business Interest Paid

Monthly checking account fees, bank overdraft penalties, business credit card finance charges, annual credit card fees and business debt interest all belong in this category.

Check all bank, credit card and loan statements for charges; this is a deduction that is often under reported.

If you take out a home equity loan to fund your business, all costs involved in getting the loan, as well as all interest charged on that loan, becomes a business deduction.

C - Cleaning Materials & Business Supplies

This category includes all work space cleaning supplies, organizing bins, light bulbs, operating supplies, coffee for clients, and all of your sales or home party supplies.

Home party supplies could include disposable plates and glasses, reusable holiday decorations purchased for parties, folding tables or chairs used only by your home party business, a party punch bowl, and any other items purchased to be used at one or more parties.

All little equipment purchases, those items costing less than $75 each, like crock pots or warming pans purchased for party plan entertaining, as well as any other party supplies not deducted elsewhere belong in this category.

Business supplies include any items you need to perform your job as a sales consultant, with the exception of office supplies, overhead (utilities and rent), and business equipment. Those expenses are reported in other categories.

And don't overlook those "little" items – candles, room sprays, flowers to decorate the table; these too are part of the expense of throwing a party, and therefore a deductible business expense.

Rented equipment is not included in this category. Those receipts will go with the "R" envelope – Rent Paid. Rented tables, chairs, party items, food preparation equipment or cleaning equipment all belong in "R".

D - Donations to Nonprofit Organizations

All small business donations are taken on your personal tax return; they do not go on your Schedule C business return.

Donations of goods or artwork with a value of $5,000 or more must include a qualified appraisal for each item donated. You only need an appraisal summary, unless the value exceeds $20,000, then you need the complete appraisal.

Some donations can be considered advertising expense. If you make a donation for the express purpose of promoting your business it should be deducted on your Schedule C as advertising.

Your time is not deductible as a donation; if you pay someone and donate their labor that expense is deductible. Products donated are deducted at cost as removed from inventory.

E - Educational Seminars & Classes

Seminars and classes that will help make you better at what you do to produce income, as well as general business classes, are all deductible.

Remember to record all mileage or travel expenses if you have them; those will be reported along with other mileage and travel expenses. If you only have one receipt for all, simply make copies for other expense categories and highlight the deductions that should be taken there.

If the company whose product you sell has an annual sales convention where sales classes are taught and new products are unveiled, your attendance would be deducted as an educational expense.

A business class taken at the local college would also be deducted here.

F - Fix-it & Repair Expenses

Equipment repairs, the cost involved in fixing a broken party chair, and all other repair or fix-it expenses go in this category.

If you pay a computer expert to solve a computer problem so that you can go online for order processing, that's a fix-it expense. When someone comes out to repair the bubble machine or popcorn cart you use at parties, that expense is deducted here as well.

G - Gifts

Each year you can deduct up to $25 per client or vendor, when you give gifts to that client or vendor. Make a note on the back of the receipt for the item given, and add the receiver's name.

Cookies and candy put out for all customers who visit your office are not gifts; those are business supplies and belong in category "C".

Meals you take part in do not count as gifts, they are deducted as meals. If you give a client a restaurant gift card, that would be deducted as a gift. Items taken from your inventory are not deducted as gifts either, those are deducted as inventory, on a cost per item basis.

When you give samples of your product away, those are promotional samples, not gifts. You should deduct those items in category "A".

H – Home Office Expenses

If you use one room or more in your home exclusively for business, you may be able to deduct a portion of your home operating expenses. This includes rent or interest and property taxes paid, plus household insurance, all shared utilities, lawn maintenance and cleaning.

Any item used 100% by the business can be 100% expensed.

How much you get to deduct for shared expenses is based on the size of your home versus the space devoted exclusively to the business.

Annual totals for each home office expense needs to be written on the front of the Home Office Expense envelope after you sort; the IRS requires that all home office expenses be listed separately.

If you own your own home, you should discuss the disadvantages of depreciating a home office with a tax professional before taking this portion of the home office deduction. Depreciation will affect taxes due when you sell your home; you will not be able to exclude the office portion of your personal residence profit from taxes.

You do not have to depreciate your home to take the other home office deductions.

I - Insurance

Business and liability insurance are expensed here. Health insurance is not. If you have self-employed health insurance costs they will be reported on the front of your 1040 personal return, not on your business tax return.

J - Job Required Licenses & Dues

Business and license fees, union dues, and membership dues paid to any professional or business networking organization are all included in category "J". If you join a networking organization for the purpose of booking parties, those dues are deductible.

L - Legal & Professional Fees

All bookkeeping, payroll service fees and legal fees incurred by your business are deductible.

Any self employed person who pays an attorney to look over a contract or prepare legal papers has expenses to deduct here.

Hiring a bookkeeping service to handle paperwork or payroll is also included in this category.

Payment for tax preparation should be included here, but only the portion that applies to your business tax return.

M - Meals & Entertainment

If you take clients or business associates out to improve your business relationship, it may be deductible. You must always note the client or associate's name on the back of the receipt, as well as what business you discussed. Business meals are only 50% deductible.

Meals eaten during overnight travel need to be totaled separately. The IRS per diem rates are often a better way to expense travel meals; the per diem method requires less work but can only be applied to overnight travel meals.

Entertainment expenses included in this category are those that you attended along with your client. This could be anything from a baseball game to opera; as long as you take that client or vendor for the purpose of improving your business relationship.

If you do not attend, but merely give tickets to a vendor or client, those tickets would be categorized as a gift or promotional expense, and those receipts sorted to "G" if gifts or "A" if promotion. Consider the $25 rule before classifying entertainment as a gift.

Example #1: *Jenna buys a block of tickets to the annual bridal show, and gives them to people who are engaged and planning their wedding. She does this because she wants them to come see the Bridal Baskets and Mother-of-the-Bride gifts offered by the company that she represents*

Jenna is trying to sell her product, and that makes those tickets a promotional expense, not an entertainment expense.

Example #2: *Judy sells scrapbook supplies and signs up to attend a 2010 national bridal show 300 miles away from home. In exchange for teaching some classes, she gets a booth where she can sell product during this 10-day event. Judy kept her apartment while she was gone, and stayed in a hotel while working the event.*

Her travel and motel expenses will end up in the Travel envelope, but all meal receipts for those 10 nights that Judy spent at the show location need to be lumped together in the meal category, with a notation about the length of time spent away from home on this out of town show.

When Judy's taxes were prepared, the 2010 standard meal allowance rate for overnight trips was $46 a day in most U.S. cities. Rather than add up all of the fast food, restaurant and drive-thru coffee stand receipts Judy had, plus her notes about late-night stops at convenience stores for food and snacks she remembered, but had no receipts for, her accountant simply multiplied $46 times 10 days. Then he took half of that $460 standard meal allowance for a deduction of $230.

N - Newspapers, Magazines & Subscriptions

Magazines, newspapers and newsletters that you purchase to enhance your business knowledge belong in this category. They do not have to be printed; online subscriptions count as well.

This includes magazines you read to stay current on business trends, industry changes or other aspects of your business. The herb and truck gardener could deduct gardening subscriptions, the dog breeder specialty dog magazines, and everyone could deduct a subscription on business operating procedures.

O - Office Supplies

Office supplies are different from business supplies. Business supplies are specific to your trade or industry; office supplies are used by all small businesses. Dictionaries and office reference books, paper, photocopies, adding machine tape, computer supplies, paper clips, staples, pens, notepads, appointment books, and other desk or office supplies belong here. The cost of this organizer can be included in this category since it tames the paperwork.

If you pay another business to send your faxes, that too is an office supply expense.

P - People Who Take a Share

You only use this category if your payments are processed by an agent who takes a cut of the total before issuing your payment, or if you are required to pay a fee to someone who sells your services or product.

This is not the way home party sales consultants work, so you will not need this envelope.

If you host parties and sell products for one of the major cosmetic, scrapbook, vitamin or other corporations who promotes door to door sales and/or home parties as tools for growing your business, you will have nothing in this envelope.

Even if your plan pays you a percentage of the sales made by someone else, perhaps a new sales rep that you signed up, you will not use this category. All of those commissions will be accounted for in your income deposits.

If you receive a statement showing commissions simple store it with your other tax records.

Q- Equipment Purchased

Any furniture or equipment you buy for your business, including desks, file cabinets, computers, camera, calculator, printer, desk lamp, waiting area couch, office artwork, display equipment, etc., must be expensed over its expected life.

Tax Pro Rule #5

Any equipment purchased,

with an expected life of two or more years

must be depreciated or expensed

as a Section 179 deduction.

The general rule is, if it will be used for two or more years, and cost over $75, it will need to go here, for a depreciation deduction.

In most cases you can deduct the entire expense all at once; using a technique the IRS calls the Section 179 deduction.

Your tax professional will need to know the date of purchase, and cost of each tool or piece of equipment you buy, for your business tax return. Itemize all purchases on the outside of this envelope when you sort, including all of the information required.

R - Rent Paid

If you are buying your office building you will include all interest paid on the mortgage in this category. Post this information on the front of the "R" envelope. If you pay rent for an office or storage space, rent tools or equipment, pay for loft space, or have other rent expenses, include all of those costs in this category. Home office expenses do not belong in this category; the go in the "H" envelope.

S - Shipping & Postage

Stamps purchased to send out business mail, as well as any UPS, FedEx or other shipping or transport fees paid to send out products or business materials belong in the "S" envelope.

Many independent business people use personal stamps to send out business bills. Buy your own stamps and take the deduction. You'll be surprised at how fast those stamps mount up, and by deducting every little business expense allowed and spent, you increase your profit.

If you pay shipping to receive an item purchased for inventory, that shipping expense will be included with inventory expenses.

T - Travel

All business trips and seminar travel expenses, including airfare, tips, taxi or bus, parking, entry fees, and hotel expenses are deductible travel expenses.

Taking your spouse along for pleasure does not make his or her portion of the trip deductible; only your portion will be deductible. If a trip includes both business and pleasure days, only a portion of the travel expenses can be deducted.

Overnight business trip meals are also deductible, but need to be listed as a separate total for proper reporting.

If you are away overnight often, write the total number of nights you spent out of town on the front of this envelope, as well as the total spent for overnight travel meals when you sort.

Put the actual travel meal receipts with the "M" envelope; clip them together and tag them overnight meal receipts, keeping them separate from other meal receipts.

If you travel a lot, when your taxes are prepared ask your tax preparer if the IRS per diem rate established for meal deductions would be a better way for you to expense your overnight meals.

U - Utilities

If you rent a shop or office space and pay utilities they are deducted here. This includes the electricity, water, internet fees, heat, garbage, office telephone, and cable or music subscription fees used at the office.

All business long distance telephone charges, the cost of a 2nd telephone line at home, or a cell phone, that is used exclusively for business can be deducted here. The cost of your primary household telephone is not deductible, even if you use it for business.

Home office utilities do not go in this envelope; they belong in the "H" envelope.

V - Vehicle (Car & Truck) Expenses

If you keep good mileage records you'll pay less tax. That's because for every 100 miles you drive for your business you get to subtract around $50 as an expense.

Tax Pro Rule #6

Unless you have a vehicle used only for business,

keep a notebook in the car

and write down every business mile.

Business miles include every trip you make to pick up business or office supplies, drop off business mail, transport a client, or attend professional classes or seminars. The little trips to drop bills at the post office or run to the office supply store for paper add up quickly, and, with the cost of gas you don't want to miss any business miles you drive. The deduction can be huge, depending on how much you drive.

If you kept a mileage log whenever you ran business errands, simply add up your mileage log and use that total for your deductible business miles. Your total vehicle miles can be approximated, if you have your actual business miles written down.

Write the total miles driven for your business on the front of the "V" envelope.

If you are able to devote one vehicle exclusively to your business, all you need are the odometer numbers at the beginning of year (BOY) and the end of year (EOY). If you took the mileage deduction last year, that EOY mileage figure on last year's tax return will become your BOY figure for this year.

If this is your first year in business, and you didn't write the opening mileage down at the start of your business year, check repair or oil change receipts, they may show your mileage, and figure it out from there.

If more than half of all miles put on a vehicle are business related miles, you should also track actual vehicle expenses to see if this is a better deduction. To take actual vehicle expenses or depreciate your vehicle, you will need to itemize all of the vehicle's expenses on the front of the "V" envelope and save all receipts. Actual vehicle expenses might include car payments, repair costs, tires or parts purchased, auto insurance, vehicle registration fees, gas, oil, and any other costs involved in operating that vehicle.

If you use more than one vehicle in your business, keep track of miles driven in each vehicle. Note each vehicle's miles separately on the front of this expense envelope.

W- Wages & Contract Labor Expenses

If you have employees, find a quality bookkeeping service; most will handle all of the regulatory paperwork for a small fee. Payroll requires regular deposits of taxes withheld as well as deposits of matching sums.

Most small business owners don't have the time to add payroll to their "to do" list; lots of qualified bookkeeping companies offer this service.

At the end of the year they can furnish payroll reports showing where all of the money went that did not go directly to the employee. You will need these numbers when your tax return is prepared; put all payroll reports in the "W" envelope, after writing totals on the front.

When you use independent contractors, who are not incorporated, the IRS requires you to file a 1099M form reporting all earnings paid to each person, if you pay them $600 or more during the tax year.

These forms can be purchased at any office supply store and must be put in the mail by January 31st. A copy is also sent to the IRS.

If you get caught avoiding payroll taxes by claiming an employee as an independent contractor, the IRS can fine you heavily, and make you pay all unpaid taxes, even those normally paid by the employee.

Someone who works exclusively for you, on your time schedule, doing a job exactly the way you instruct, using your tools or office space, is probably not an independent contractor.

You may have an employee, even if they only work a few hours a week, which means you are required to classify them as an employee and follow all laws regarding payroll.

If you're confused about the difference between an independent contractor and an employee, discuss this with a tax professional. An error here now could be expensive later.

X - Taxes & Business Licenses

The letter T was already used and taxes are by law required to be eXact and so "X" was chosen to represent taxes. This is where you enter all state sales taxes, city taxes and any other taxes paid for your business.

Don't forget to record your quarterly federal and/or state income tax installment payments. If you pay property taxes on your business building, they too belong here.

Any license required by the state, county or city to operate a business, or practice your profession, also gets sorted into this category. Your vehicle license does not belong here. If you are expensing your vehicle the license receipt would go with other vehicle expenses.

Z - Inventory

Most self-employed people do not have inventory. The IRS considers any item you make or purchase for resale inventory. Items purchased for a particular customer, and items you buy to complete a job are not inventory.

Tax Pro Rule #7

All items purchased or created for resale,

are considered inventory by the IRS.

Inventory expenses can only be deducted

as that inventory is sold.

Inventory expenses are deducted on a cost per item basis, and not deducted completely, until every item is sold or removed from inventory. As you sort through receipts, pull every receipt that has anything to do with inventory, including shipping charges, and put them into this category.

If you only host parties for one company, all you need are the invoices received for each shipment. Put them in date order with the invoices for December on top. On the last day of December count all inventory on your shelves and write those items down.

Starting with the last invoice showing product received in December, look for each item remaining in inventory on those invoices. As you find items on those receipts that are remaining on your shelves, highlight those items on the invoices.

Put all other invoices aside; we're concerned only with those invoices containing highlighted product for now. That is because you need to find the value of all items that you have left in inventory on those invoices, before putting them away with the other invoices. Read the examples that follow to learn more about putting a value on inventory.

Total the value of all goods remaining on your shelves. Write this number down as your **end of year inventory value.**

Total your entire stack of inventory receipts, including those with highlighted items. The sum of all of your inventory receipts is the **total value of all inventory purchased.**

Subtract the value of your end-of-year inventory from the total value of all inventory purchased, and you will know how much you can deduct for inventory sold. This number is referred to as your **inventory expense.**

Sorting Your Expense Receipts

Once you understand the categories, and have your expense envelopes labeled, lay those 24 envelopes out on an empty table or desk. Eliminate any envelopes that you know you will not use. For example, you may not have inventory, home office deductions, people who take a share, or meal expenses; which would take 4 envelopes off the table.

Space the remaining envelopes far enough apart to avoid mixing paperwork when you sort.

Now you are ready to begin sorting.

Go through all of your receipts, one by one, and decide where each receipt belongs. Lay the receipt on top of the proper expense envelope. Some receipts could be classified in more than one way; unless this book states otherwise just choose the one you think fits best.

To make the sort go quicker, put anything you cannot immediately classify into a "second run" pile. After sorting all of the easy receipts, go back to that stack and try again.

Any that you can't figure out, simply clip together; they can be dealt with individually when your taxes are prepared.

If you run inventory, don't forget to put all expenses involved in receiving and producing that inventory on top of the "Z" envelope, even though it may also qualify for another category.

Generally, all business expenses will easily fall into one of the 24 expense categories.

Posting Business Deductions

In Step Three you will post all of those envelope totals onto one sheet of paper. For now, set the Inventory envelope aside. Inventory expenses are explained separately, as they are handled differently.

Add up all of the receipts in each category and write the total on the front of the envelope. Once you have written the total on an envelope, tuck the receipts inside. You will not need to open that envelope again, unless you later find an additional receipt.

If you discover additional receipts, simply scratch out the old total and write the new total on the envelope and put those receipts inside. You will need to change the total anywhere else you have posted it as well.

When you're all done with your taxes, you'll store all of these expense envelopes in a bag or box marked Tax Receipts. Rules for keeping tax receipts and storage tips are addressed in the final chapter of this book.

If you have used sheets of paper instead of envelopes, fold them in half to create your own pocket envelope, and staple, glue or tape three edges together. Put your receipts inside and staple closed. Make sure to fold the paper with your totals on the outside.

Tracking Inventory

When new inventory is added, a "per item" cost must be calculated. This is computed by dividing the total cost to add that item to inventory by the number of items added.

You will need to count all remaining inventory at the close of each tax year, and keep inventory records, if you want to survive an audit.

If you do not have inventory items, you may want to skip the rest of this section on how to manage business inventory.

Here are a few real-life examples of how inventory costs are calculated.

Example #1: *Jenica received shipments from the company she sold scrapbook supplies for at least once a month. Once she had gathered all of her receipts, with the newest invoice on top, she made a list of all the scrapbook supplies that still remained on her shelves. She had 14 different items; only 1-2 remained of some things, but she had 4-7 of others, and a dozen of one.*

On the first invoice Jenica found all of the single unit items. She highlighted the invoice entries, writing 1 and circling it in front of the highlight, and checked those items off her inventory list. She also found 10 of a decoration her inventory showed 12 of in stock. She highlighted those 10, crossed off the 12 on her list, and wrote 2 as the new missing total.

When Jenica located the final 2 items they were part of a 30-like-item purchase. To find the value of those 2 remaining in stock, she had to divide the total cost by 30 to know what each item cost, and then multiply that single-item cost times 2.

Going thru the rest of the invoices she quickly located the other items still in inventory, and marked them off the same way she had done the others. Once she had totaled the cost of all remaining inventory, she had the value of her end-of-year inventory.

By subtracting the value of the inventory that remained on her shelves from the total cost of all inventory purchased, Jenica quickly knew how much she had spent on inventory, and what she could take as a deductible expense.

The value of Jenica's end of year inventory is also her opening inventory value for the following tax year.

Example #4: *Sharon fell in love with a line of specialty scrapbooking paper and signed on to sell the paper to friends and family through home party sales. She got off to a good start with a huge order at her first party.*

She paid the company $900 for her initial order and $2400 for her second order. Samples were not included in this purchase. Add those figures together to get total inventory costs of $3300.

Sharon got 1800 packages of paper, each containing 10 sheets, for that $3300. If you divide that $3300 by 1800 you will get $1.83 per package.

If Sharon sells 600 packages of paper that first year she will deduct $1098.00. The balance will not be deducted until the rest of the packets of paper are sold or disposed of by Sharon.

However, Sharon's mother was injured in an automobile accident before the year ended and Sharon decided to move back home to help her father to care for her during her recovery. She knew she could not handle a new business at the same time, and decided to donate the rest of the inventory.

Before she left town, Sharon gave the remaining 1200 packets of paper to the local high school for use in their art classes. Because she disposed of those additional 1200 packages of paper she can deduct the entire cost.

There is no donation benefit since you can only deduct what you pay for an item.

Creating a New Inventory Report

To track new inventory you will need to create a New Inventory Report.

Turn to the next empty page in your notebook and write "New Inventory Report" across the top.

Draw seven vertical columns, with the first column being wider than any of the last six. Label those seven columns across the top as follows:

(1) Product Name & Quantity

(2) Total Cost

(3) Cost per Item

(4) # Removed from Inventory

(5) Value of Inventory Removed

(6) End of Year Inventory

(7) EOY Inventory Value

Filling out a New Inventory Report

In Column (1) enter the Product Name and how many saleable items you initially put into inventory.

Column (2) will include every penny you spent to produce or obtain that product.

To get this figure you will add all of your material and production expenses together. Depending on the inventory item, you may have parts invoices, delivery expenses, outside labor, vendor invoices, or other costs. Enter this total in Column (2).

The number in Column (3) is obtained by dividing the Total Cost (2) by Product Quantity (1).

In future years, enter all new inventory on a New Inventory Report Sheet as it arrives, completing columns 1-3 at that time. You can fill out the rest of the columns on the last work day of the year, when you count the end of year inventory.

In Column (4) enter how many of this item were sold, given away as samples, destroyed or donated; in other words every item removed from your saleable inventory during the tax year.

To determine this number complete your inventory count for column 6 and subtract the opening inventory count for the year.

Column (5) is figured by multiplying Column (3) x Column (4). That is the value assigned to all of the items sold this year, and will be the amount you get to deduct from your income.

Inventory is always counted on the last working day of the tax year. Simply count the items remaining in stock, both in your office as well as items unsold in a distributor's inventory, and enter that number in Column (6).

Column (7) is figured by multiplying Column (3) x Column (6).

Column (5) contains the total cost of items sold, and is the amount you can deduct from this year's inventory expense.

Creating a Prior Year Inventory Report

If this is not your first year with inventory, you will also need a Prior Year Inventory Report. This is where you record all inventory carried forward from the last tax year into the current tax year.

To create this report, begin by writing "Prior Year Inventory Report" across the top of the page. Then draw 6 vertical columns and label them as follows:

(1) Product Name & BOY Inventory

(2) Cost per Item

(3) # Removed from Inventory

(4) Value of Inventory Removed

(5) End of Year Inventory

(6) EOY Inventory Value

Filling out a Prior Year Inventory Report

In Column (1) enter the Product Name and how many saleable items remained in inventory at the beginning of the tax year.

Column (2) is the same cost per item dollar amount you used to report inventory sold in prior years. Enter the Cost per Item in the second column.

The number in Column (3) reflects how many of this product you sold, gave away as samples, destroyed or donated. You can determine this figure by counting the inventory remaining at the end of the year and subtracting that from the opening inventory for the same year.

Column (4) is determined by multiplying Column (2) x Column (3). That is the total value assigned to all sales of this particular item, and will be the amount you get to deduct off your tax return.

On the last day of the tax year, count all remaining inventory and enter that number in Column (5).

Column (6) is determined by multiplying Column (2) x Column (5). This is the total deductible value of inventory remaining unsold.

You'll learn how to deduct those inventory expenses in the next chapter. Once you have the details posted to the reports in your notebook, you can write new and prior year inventory totals on the front of the Inventory envelope, and put all inventory receipts inside. Set the Inventory envelope aside, with the Income envelope; you won't need it again unless you're audited.

STEP THREE: PUTTING IT ALL TOGETHER

This final step has you posting all of the expense totals you've written on the front of the expense envelopes, and other figures you've already transferred to your notebook, onto a few final notebook pages.

When you're done, this last report will contain all of the information you or a tax professional will need to prepare your small business Schedule C tax return.

What to take to the Tax Professional

A tax professional can only work from the information you provide, and unless you know a little bit about business taxes even a good tax professional can miss valuable deductions.

Tax Pro Rule #8

No matter how good your tax professional is,

if you don't provide

all of the necessary information and figures,

your tax return will be wrong.

You've already learned a lot, and by the time you finish this book you'll know enough to do your own simple Schedule C tax return if you choose. But, unless you have a thorough understanding of accounting it may not be the best approach, especially if you intend to depreciate your vehicle or new equipment.

Most people leave the tax professional's office each year knowing nothing more about tax law than they did the year before. When you visit the tax pro, ask questions, and if he or she cannot answer your questions go elsewhere.

When you visit that professional, take along all of your personal income tax information, because your business profit or loss is simply posted to your personal 1040 tax return before it is filed. The tax professional will complete all supporting tax forms.

Have your taxes prepared as early in the year as possible. When you owe taxes, the money is not due until April 15th, even if you mail your tax return on January 2nd. And remember, not all taxes are bad. Self-employment taxes fund your Social Security and Medicare, and if you don't pay much in, you won't draw much out during your senior years.

Deducting that Home Office

If you have a home office, you'll need to take the following figures to your tax preparer as well:

- Total square footage of your home. This can be found in your home purchase or rental documents.

- Total square footage of the total area used exclusively for business. Multiply the room length times the room width; if more than one room is used add those sums together.

- Total annual amount paid for household insurance rent, repairs and lawn maintenance, utilities (electricity, water, sewer, gas, and garbage) and other household expenses that your home and business shared. If you had any expenses that were 100% home office related list those separately. You will also need mortgage interest and real estate 1099's if you own your home.

Go to the next empty page in your notebook and label it Home Office Deductions. Enter all of this information on that page.

If you choose to depreciate your home office space you should see a tax professional first.

Depreciating a home office could be a 30 year tax project, and when the house is eventually sold you will have to exclude that portion of gain from the personal residence tax shelter. Unless you know the tax laws on depreciation, this is not something an individual should tackle themselves.

If you remodel your office or home, re-roof the structure, create a separate office entrance, or make any other changes that also affect the business portion of your home, you can depreciate the business portion of those expenses as well. If you have any of these expenses, be sure to include that information on this notebook page as well, and discuss them with your tax professional.

Creating an Annual Tax Report

Keep that notebook handy, because you need one final form. This is where you will combine all of your totals into one end-of-year report. Write ANNUAL TAX REPORT, followed by the tax year, across the top of the next empty page.

There are no columns needed on this form, simply enter your information line-by-line.

Label the first line, on the left hand side of the paper, TOTAL GROSS INCOME. Turn to the first page in your notebook, the one labeled Business Income, and look for the amount you wrote down as Total Gross Income. Enter that number on the first line of the Annual Tax Report. If you have broken out any income to be listed separately, like barter income, write this down under OTHER INCOME.

Leave a little space before writing TOTAL ANNUAL EXPENSES on the left side of the page.

Below this list the Business Expense Alphabet, letter by letter. Place a dollar sign after each listing except the last one; when you get to Z (Inventory) write YES if you have inventory, NO if you don't. Leave a little extra space if an expense category requires a breakdown of expenses.

Your Annual Tax Report sheet will look something like the one on the following two pages.

ANNUAL TAX REPORT (20__)

Total Gross Income $____________

Other Income $____________

TOTAL ANNUAL EXPENSES

A - Advertising & Promotional Expenses $____________

B – Bank/Visa/Other Business Interest Paid $____________

C - Cleaning Materials & Business Supplies $____________

D - Donations to Nonprofit Organizations $____________

E - Educational Seminars & Classes $____________

F - Fix-it & Repair Expenses $____________

G - Gifts $____________

H – Home Office Expenses:

Breakdown: Mortgage principle, property tax, insurance, utilities and other expenses.

I - Insurance $____________

J - Job Required Licenses & Dues $____________

L - Legal & Professional Fees $____________

M - Meals & Entertainment: Total dollars $____________

N – Newspapers, Magazines & Subscriptions $____________

O - Office Supplies $____________

P - People Who Take a Share $____________

Q - Equipment Purchased $____________

Breakdown: List all new equipment, date purchased and amount spent.

R - Rent Paid $____________

S - Shipping & Postage $____________

T - Travel: Non-meal Expenses $____________

Breakdown: Travel meals - include number of nights spent away from home.

U - Utilities $____________

V - Vehicle (Car & Truck) Total Expenses $____________

Breakdown #1: Total Business Miles on Calendar

Breakdown #2: List all vehicle expenses if depreciating vehicle

W - Wages & Contract Labor Expenses $____________

Breakdown: W-2 and 1099 worker costs.

X - Taxes & Business Licenses $____________

Z - Inventory – YES or NO

Now, that you have the Annual Tax Report ready, transfer the total you wrote on the front of each expense envelope onto this report. This will be the dollar figure you got by totaling all receipts in that category, before you tucked the receipts inside. If you need other information, it too will be found on the outside of the envelope, if you followed the instructions on sorting and totaling.

This is the bulk of the information you, or your tax professional, will need in order to add your self-employed business tax return to your personal 1040.

If you paid any taxes in advance, generally referred to as Estimated Quarterly Taxesto either the state or federal government, don't forget to note how much you paid to each entity, and when those payments were made. These payments are credited on your 1040 personal return.

If you have payroll expenses, take all payroll reports and copies of any payroll tax forms filed to your tax professional. Stick all of this paperwork in the back of the notebook so you'll have it all together when you need it.

If you have a ***simple*** business return, and ***always*** prepare your own personal tax return, the following chapter on preparing your own Schedule C tax return will help. It walks you through the process line-by-line, showing you where to post all of the information on your Annual Tax Report.

No one without accounting knowledge should attempt a tax return with depreciation.

Equipment with a longer life than one year must be tracked for the lifetime of the item, and has complicated rules; and that is why depreciation is best left for tax professionals and accountants.

The majority of independent contractors take depreciation deductions all at once by using the Section 179 deduction. This book only explains how to take the Section 179 option, deducting the entire expense the year of purchase.

If you want to depreciate your car or truck, instead of taking the standard mileage deduction, you are also no longer preparing a simple Schedule C tax return. Depreciation is confusing, even for tax professionals, and the rules change often. Vehicle depreciation instructions are not included in this guide. However, the standard mileage deduction includes depreciation.

This organizer's chapter on *Developing an Audit-Proof Mindset* explains what to do with all of the tax records you've organized, and how to develop an audit-proof mindset. If you don't intend to do your own taxes, you can turn to page 77 now.

PREPARING A SMALL BUSINESS TAX RETURN

Not everyone should be doing their own taxes. Even those who are qualified would be smart to make an appointment with a tax professional for advice on tax planning every 3-5 years; just to learn what's new.

Any time you experience major changes in your business or personal life, you should consult with a tax professional for guidance. Making major decisions without considering the tax consequences can be expensive.

The following example is just one of the many common scenarios that can cost you money, if you don't know the current tax laws.

Example: *Mary has held her job with a large corporation for the past 15 years, and now has the opportunity to buy the home she has been renting for 6 years. It would be her first home. The price is right; she has her down payment in the bank, and wants to close the deal.*

Mary really wants to buy the house, but she is worried because once she empties her savings account for the down payment, she will have nothing to draw from in case of an emergency.

If Mary sat down with a tax professional, the first question would probably be ... do you have any retirement funds with the corporation that employs you, or an IRA that you can tap?

Most retirement accounts can be used as down payment for first-time home buyers, without paying the 10% Early Withdrawal Penalty. That means Mary can leave her cash in the bank, and tap her retirement account for the down payment.

With proper planning, Mary might even be able to offset most of the federal and state income taxes owed when retirement money is withdrawn.

Buying the property in early January, and paying attention to how the sale is structured, can get Mary a larger Schedule A deduction, cancelling out retirement income gains.

Tax Pro Rule #9

Tax laws change every year,

sometimes offering huge tax savings for

only a short time. Even if you do your own taxes,

it is wise to speak with a tax pro occasionally,

just to keep up on new tax credits

and tax planning opportunities.

Introducing Schedule C - The Small Business Tax Form

IRS Form Schedule C is where all small business income and expenses are reported. This tax form is not submitted separately, but is filed along with your personal tax return, and the net profit or loss from this schedule is posted to your 1040 tax form.

Any individual or married couple operating a small business will use this form; corporations and un-married partnerships do not use this form.

If you have less than $5,000 worth of expenses, and they appear in only a couple of categories, you may be able to use Schedule C-EZ.

Small business owners who establish a corporate structure merely for financial protection may still end up filing their business taxes on a Schedule C. Ask the professional who helped you to set up your corporation if you're not sure which form to file.

If you have more than one business, and they are not related, you will need to fill out more than one Schedule C. A vitamin sales consultant who also sells water purification products for another company can include all income and expenses on one Schedule C. A vitamin sales consultant who also does automotive repair would need a separate Schedule C for the repair business.

This chapter is designed to walk you through the actual preparation of your Schedule C return, line-by-line.

Sit down with the notebook that contains the reports you created and your tax forms; it's just a matter of transferring the information as instructed.

Completing a Schedule C Tax Form

Schedule C, and any other tax forms you need, can be downloaded at www.IRS.gov. To get the current year's Schedule C, simply click on Forms and Publications, and then click on Schedule C to print or download.

A sample copy of the complete Schedule C tax form appears in Appendix A.

The following pages will explain where to post all of the income, expenses and other details you wrote in your spiral notebook. These instructions are written so that you can sit down with your tax form and move line by line, dropping in numbers as directed.

Whenever you're supposed to write information on a particular line of your tax form, that line number or heading will be all in CAPITAL letters, to help you to focus on where you're supposed to write your information.

Instructions for supporting forms you will need to complete a simple business return are also included.

Now let's work on that Schedule C, section by section. An illustration of the top portion appears below.

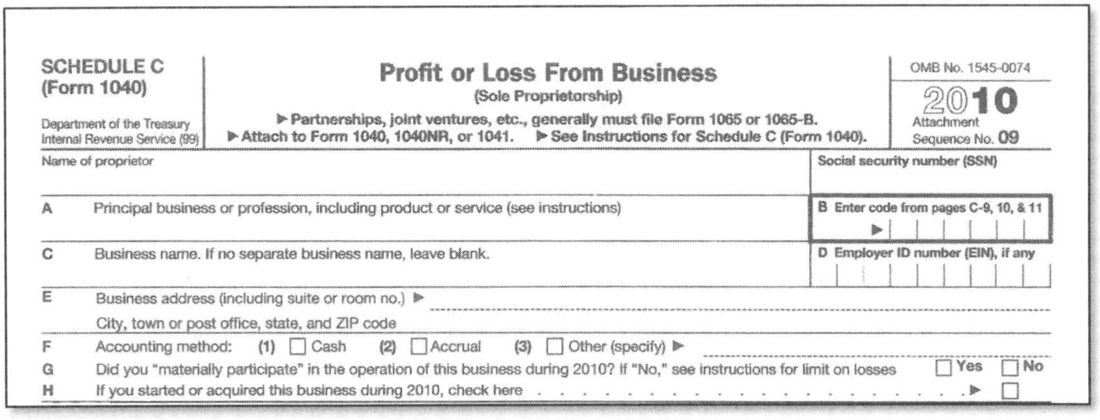

SCHEDULE C (Form 1040)
Department of the Treasury Internal Revenue Service (99)

Profit or Loss From Business
(Sole Proprietorship)
▶ Partnerships, joint ventures, etc., generally must file Form 1065 or 1065-B.
▶ Attach to Form 1040, 1040NR, or 1041. ▶ See Instructions for Schedule C (Form 1040).

OMB No. 1545-0074
2010
Attachment Sequence No. 09

Name of proprietor | Social security number (SSN)

A Principal business or profession, including product or service (see instructions) | B Enter code from pages C-9, 10, & 11 ▶

C Business name. If no separate business name, leave blank. | D Employer ID number (EIN), if any

E Business address (including suite or room no.) ▶
City, town or post office, state, and ZIP code

F Accounting method: (1) ☐ Cash (2) ☐ Accrual (3) ☐ Other (specify) ▶

G Did you "materially participate" in the operation of this business during 2010? If "No," see instructions for limit on losses ☐ Yes ☐ No

H If you started or acquired this business during 2010, check here . . . ▶ ☐

Begin by filling in the self-employed person's name in the box marked **PROPRIETOR**; put their **SOCIAL SECURITY NUMBER** in the box at the end of the line.

LINE A is where you will write your profession – independent sales consultant, party plan merchandiser, or whatever title your company uses to refer to the men and women in their sales force.

You can actually enter any title that you feel fits what you do for a living best – party rep, sales coordinator, wedding scrapbooker, home party sales, or any other professional title you have chosen to represent the work that you do.

This is followed by the business code for your industry.

The code to write on **LINE B** is 454390; this represents direct selling consultants and sales people, including door-to-door sales reps, frozen food plan providers and party plan merchandisers.

LINE C is left empty if you operate your business in your personal name. Otherwise fill in your business name here.

If you have obtained an EIN (Employer Identification Number), you can add this number on **LINE D**.

If you work out of your home leave **LINE E** empty. If you have an office address put it on this line.

Most independent business men and women operate on a CASH BASIS. That means you deduct an expense when it occurs, whether you pay in cash or get a bill, and count income the day it arrives in the mail.

The accrual system is complicated and used by larger businesses. Put an X in the cash box on **LINE F** unless you have an accountant, and then ask your accountant which system you use, it's probably cash.

LINE G is marked YES, unless you do not participate in your own business; this is something party plan and door-to-door sales consultants are required to do, actively participate.

LINE H is only checked on the first year that you operate your business. If this is your first Schedule C for this business check this box now.

Now flip the form over and fill out the backside. The back of your Schedule C needs to be filled out before you can continue with the front.

The top portion of the back, shown below, begins with Part III – Cost of Goods Sold. This is where you will enter any inventory figures.

If you do not have inventory skip Part III, and move on to Part IV of this form; those instructions begin on the following page.

Part III **Cost of Goods Sold** (see instructions)

33	Method(s) used to value closing inventory: a ☐ Cost b ☐ Lower of cost or market c ☐ Other (attach explanation)		
34	Was there any change in determining quantities, costs, or valuations between opening and closing inventory? If "Yes," attach explanation . . . ☐ Yes ☐ No		
35	Inventory at beginning of year. If different from last year's closing inventory, attach explanation . . .	35	
36	Purchases less cost of items withdrawn for personal use . . .	36	
37	Cost of labor. Do not include any amounts paid to yourself . . .	37	
38	Materials and supplies . . .	38	
39	Other costs . . .	39	
40	Add lines 35 through 39 . . .	40	
41	Inventory at end of year . . .	41	
42	**Cost of goods sold.** Subtract line 41 from line 40. Enter the result here and on page 1, line 4 . . .	42	

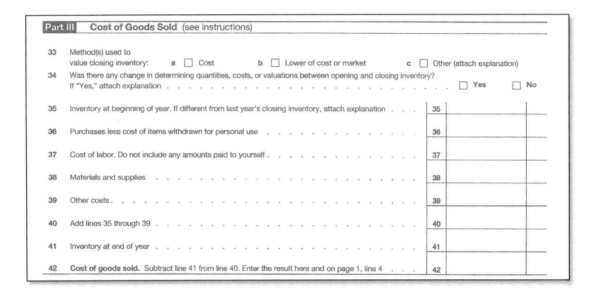

If you have inventory mark the first box on **LINE 33** with an X, showing that your inventory is valued at its cost.

If you valued it in a different manner last year check yes on **LINE 34**, otherwise mark the box marked NO.

Enter your beginning of the year inventory value on **LINE 35**; if you had no inventory at the start of the tax year put a zero in this box.

LINE 36 is where you enter the cost of all new inventory added during this tax year. You will find that figure by adding everything in Column 2 of the New Inventory Report you created earlier.

Labor, materials and supplies, and other expenses can be broken out and listed separately, but this is not required. Yours were added into inventory. Skipping Lines 37-39, write the number you posted on Line 36 onto **LINE 40**.

Going back to the New and Prior Year Inventory Reports in your notebook, add all the end of year inventory values together and place that total on **LINE 41**.

Subtract Line 41 from Line 40 and you will have the Cost of Goods Sold; enter this on **LINE 42**.

The back of the Schedule C also includes two sections titled Part IV - Information on Your Vehicle and Part V - Other Expenses. Those two sections are illustrated below.

Part IV **Information on Your Vehicle.** Complete this part **only** if you are claiming car or truck expenses on line 9 and are not required to file Form 4562 for this business. See the instructions for line 13 to find out if you must file Form 4562.

43 When did you place your vehicle in service for business purposes? (month, day, year) ▶ ___ / ___ / ___

44 Of the total number of miles you drove your vehicle during 2010, enter the number of miles you used your vehicle for:

a Business ________ b Commuting (see instructions) ________ c Other ________

45 Was your vehicle available for personal use during off-duty hours? . . . . . ☐ Yes ☐ No

46 Do you (or your spouse) have another vehicle available for personal use?. . . . . ☐ Yes ☐ No

47a Do you have evidence to support your deduction? . . . . . ☐ Yes ☐ No

b If "Yes," is the evidence written? . . . . . ☐ Yes ☐ No

Part V **Other Expenses.** List below business expenses not included on lines 8–26 or line 30.

If you use your personal vehicle, and only deduct mileage, you will need to fill out Part IV. The mileage deduction is generally around $.50 per mile driven for business use, so even if you only drive a few miles on business errands it's well worth noting.

If you want to depreciate your vehicle, you are no longer preparing a simple Schedule C tax return. Depreciation is confusing, even for some tax professionals, and the rules change often.

Depreciation instructions are not included in this guide.

If you are only taking the mileage deduction, on **LINE 43** write in the date your vehicle was brought into your business and placed in service, even if this date is from a prior year.

If this is your primary employment, you will not be allowed to deduct your commuting mileage. Getting to and from a person's primary job is not deductible.

Any mileage incurred in travelling from job one to job two is deductible, but going home after job two is not, unless it is farther from home than your primary job, then you can deduct those extra miles.

Enter all business miles on **LINE 44-a**, and all non-business miles, including non-deductible commute miles, on **LINE 44-b**.

Answer the questions on **LINES 45-47**. If you can't check the YES box on Line 47-b, you can't take a mileage deduction, so keep written records of all mileage.

Part V – **OTHER EXPENSES** is a catch-all section. Any expense that does not have a specific spot in Part II, on the front of the Schedule C, will be first listed here, totaled and eventually posted to Line 27.

If you have receipts in the expense envelopes labeled E-Education, G-Gifts, J-Job Related Licenses, N-Newspapers & Magazines, or S-Shipping, you will list each on a separate line along with the total expense. Some education expenses may also qualify for education credits on your personal 1040; check 1040 rules to see if this is a better option.

W-2 payroll expenses, but not actual wages distributed, will also be listed as Other Expenses. You'll need envelope "W" again later, but the others can be put into the "done" pile.

Now let's go back to the front of your Schedule C, to Part I, and report your business income.

Part I Income

1	Gross receipts or sales. **Caution.** See instructions and check the box if: • This income was reported to you on Form W-2 and the "Statutory employee" box on that form was checked, or • You are a member of a qualified joint venture reporting only rental real estate income not subject to self-employment tax. Also see instructions for limit on losses. ▶ ☐	1	
2	Returns and allowances	2	
3	Subtract line 2 from line 1	3	
4	Cost of goods sold (from line 42 on page 2)	4	
5	**Gross profit.** Subtract line 4 from line 3	5	
6	Other income, including federal and state gasoline or fuel tax credit or refund (see instructions)	6	
7	**Gross income.** Add lines 5 and 6 ▶	7	

On **LINE 1** enter all of your cash income - all money deposited into your bank accounts. This will include all 1099 income received.

If you refunded any money during the tax year, and this has not already been subtracted from your total income, enter that total on **LINE 2.**

Subtract Line 2 from Line 1 and enter this number on **LINE 3**; if you had no returns the number would be the same one entered on Line 1.

You have already completed the inventory section, Part III, on the back of this form. Transfer the number you wrote on Line 42, on the backside, to **LINE 4** on the front of your Schedule C.

Subtract Line 4 from Line 3 and write that number on **LINE 5**. If you had no inventory it will be the same as Line 3.

If you had barter income, rent office space or storage space to others, or had other income that you have not reported elsewhere in this section, or on your personal tax return, such as business interest income, bad debts claimed in prior years and recovered in this tax year, or equipment sold, enter that figure on **LINE 6.**

Add Line 5 and Line 6 together and write this number on **LINE 7.**

This is the Gross Income for your business. This is not your taxable business income; you must subtract expenses to arrive at that figure. So let's enter those business expenses in Part II.

Part II of Schedule C is illustrated below.

Part II **Expenses.** Enter expenses for business use of your home **only** on line 30.

8	Advertising	8	
9	Car and truck expenses (see instructions)	9	
10	Commissions and fees	10	
11	Contract labor (see instructions)	11	
12	Depletion	12	
13	Depreciation and section 179 expense deduction (not included in Part III) (see instructions)	13	
14	Employee benefit programs (other than on line 19)	14	
15	Insurance (other than health)	15	
16	Interest:		
a	Mortgage (paid to banks, etc.)	16a	
b	Other	16b	
17	Legal and professional services	17	

18	Office expense	18	
19	Pension and profit-sharing plans	19	
20	Rent or lease (see instructions):		
a	Vehicles, machinery, and equipment	20a	
b	Other business property	20b	
21	Repairs and maintenance	21	
22	Supplies (not included in Part III)	22	
23	Taxes and licenses	23	
24	Travel, meals, and entertainment:		
a	Travel	24a	
b	Deductible meals and entertainment (see instructions)	24b	
25	Utilities	25	
26	Wages (less employment credits)	26	
27	Other expenses (from line 48 on page 2)	27	

Using the Annual Tax Report you created, post the rest of your expenses in Part II. Every expense total you were instructed to write on the front of the envelopes will be posted onto this portion of the form. Simply write the total from each envelope on the matching line, unless instructed to include more information.

LINE 8 – A (Advertising & Promotional Expenses)

LINE 9 – V (Vehicle Car/Truck Expenses)

Taking the mileage deduction is easy. On the back of the Schedule C, fill out Part IV and multiply the total business miles that you entered on Line 44-a by the mileage rate allowed for the tax year. For 2011 that rate is $.51 per mile. Enter this calculation on Line 9.

Car and truck expenses can be figured in two different ways. The first method is the mileage deduction which includes average depreciation, repairs and gas. You can choose instead to depreciate your vehicle and deduct exact expenses; you will need to fill out Form 4562 to use this method.

As stated earlier, depreciation is not simple, and therefore instructions for depreciation are not included in this guide. It is best left to the tax professionals and accounting majors.

LINE 10 – P (People Who Take a Share)

LINE 11 – W (Wages & Contract Labor Expenses) Only the Contract Labor portion belongs on Line 11 – other wage expenses are posted elsewhere.

LINE 12 – Leave this line empty as it is for reporting depletion of oil and gas fields.

Equipment with a longer life than one year must be listed on IRS Form 4562 before it can be deducted. Depreciation must be tracked for the lifetime of the item, and has complicated rules; unless you have accounting training, leave depreciation for the tax pros.

Take the Section 179 option, it's easier.

If you have items in the Q envelope, they will need to be entered on Form 4562 before you can take the Section 179 deduction. You will need to refer to Form 4562 instructions for other methods of depreciation.

Stop and fill out form 4562 now. You will find the instructions on page 65.

Once you have completed Form 4562, the amount at the bottom of that form, on Line 22, is transferred to **LINE 13** on your Schedule C.

LINE 14 – W (Wages & Contract Labor Expenses) If you have W-2 employees, and you offer benefit programs such as pension or daycare, you would list those expenses on Line 14.

LINE 15 – I (Insurance)

LINE 16 a-b - B (Bank, Visa & Other Business Interest) If you are purchasing a building for your business the mortgage interest belongs on LINE 16-a; all other business interest belongs on LINE 16-b.

LINE 17 – L (Legal & Professional Fees)

LINE 18 – O (Office Supplies)

LINE 19 - If you have a pension or profit-sharing plan the dollar figure for Line 19 will be supplied by the plan administrator; a personal IRA deposit is posted to your 1040 personal tax return.

LINE 20 a-b – R (Rent Paid) Rental of office equipment, furniture or tools belongs on **LINE 20-a**; if you pay space rent that amount belongs on **LINE 20-b**.

LINE 21 – F (Fix-it & Repair Expenses)

LINE 22 – C (Cleaning Materials & Business Supplies)

LINE 23 – X (Taxes & Business Licenses)

LINE 24 a-b – T (Travel) and M (Meals & Entertainment)

Everything business travel related belongs on **LINE 24a.** All meals, even those during extended business travel, are totaled as one amount. You can deduct 50% of meal and entertainment expenses; before entering the total divide by two and put that number on **LINE 24-b**.

LINE 25 – U (Utilities) If you do not have a home office, but pay utilities for your office space, this expense will go on LINE 25.

LINE 26 – W (Wages & Contract Labor Expenses) Payroll wages are entered on Line 26.

LINE 27 is for all other expenses. Other Expenses include those in envelope E-Educational Seminars & Classes, G-Gifts, J-Job Required Licenses & Dues, N-Newspapers, Magazines & Subscriptions, S-Shipping & Postage, and any other miscellaneous expenses that could not be lumped into one of the other categories.

All of these items are first listed individually on the back of your Schedule C, under Part V - Other Expenses. Once they are itemized on the back, the grand total is posted to Line 27. Do not include home office expenses; those are dealt with in another place.

Now that all of the expenses have been posted in Part II, you will total those expenses together and enter them on the final section on the front of your Schedule C. That section is shown on the following page.

28	**Total expenses** before expenses for business use of home. Add lines 8 through 27 ▶	28	
29	Tentative profit or (loss). Subtract line 28 from line 7	29	
30	Expenses for business use of your home. Attach **Form 8829**	30	
31	**Net profit or (loss).** Subtract line 30 from line 29. • If a profit, enter on both **Form 1040, line 12,** and **Schedule SE, line 2,** or on **Form 1040NR, line 13** (if you checked the box on line 1, see instructions). Estates and trusts, enter on **Form 1041, line 3.** • If a loss, you **must** go to line 32.	31	
32	If you have a loss, check the box that describes your investment in this activity (see instructions). • If you checked 32a, enter the loss on both **Form 1040, line 12,** and **Schedule SE, line 2,** or on **Form 1040NR, line 13** (if you checked the box on line 1, see the line 31 instructions). Estates and trusts, enter on **Form 1041, line 3.** • If you checked 32b, you **must** attach **Form 6198.** Your loss may be limited.	32a ☐ All investment is at risk. 32b ☐ Some investment is not at risk.	

Begin by adding Lines 8 thru 27, your expenses in Part II, and write that total on **LINE 28.**

Subtract Line 28 from Line 7 and enter that number on **LINE 29.**

This is your tentative profit or loss. However, if you have a home office you must complete one more step before you have the final figure.

You will need to fill out Form 8829 to take the home office deduction. Stop and fill out Form 8829 now. You will find instructions on page 67.

After filling out Form 8829, return here and enter the number you put on Line 35 of Form 8829 onto your Schedule C's **LINE 30.**

Subtract Line 30 from Line 29 and enter this number on **LINE 31.** If you had a loss, that number will have a minus (-) in front of it.

If you have a loss, but are working to create profit, check **BOX 32a**; otherwise mark **BOX 32b.** If you check Box 32b your loss will be limited.

If you do not have a home office or major equipment purchases, or you have already completed Form 4562 (Depreciation) and/or Form 8829 (Home Office), you're ready to finish the job.

Instructions for Form 4562 follow; those for Form 8829 appear on page 67.

Now turn to page 71, the section on Posting Profit or Loss to your 1040 Tax Return, and let's finish your self-employment taxes.

Figuring Section 179 Deductions – Form 4562

A sample copy of the complete IRS Form 4562 appears in Appendix A.

Let's start by filling out the top portion.

Form **4562**
Department of the Treasury
Internal Revenue Service (99)

Depreciation and Amortization
(Including Information on Listed Property)
▶ See separate instructions. ▶ Attach to your tax return.

OMB No. 1545-0172
2010
Attachment Sequence No. **67**

Name(s) shown on return	Business or activity to which this form relates	Identifying number

Part I Election To Expense Certain Property Under Section 179
Note: *If you have any listed property, complete Part V before you complete Part I.*

1	Maximum amount (see instructions)	1	
2	Total cost of section 179 property placed in service (see instructions)	2	
3	Threshold cost of section 179 property before reduction in limitation (see instructions)	3	
4	Reduction in limitation. Subtract line 3 from line 2. If zero or less, enter -0-	4	
5	Dollar limitation for tax year. Subtract line 4 from line 1. If zero or less, enter -0-. If married filing separately, see instructions	5	

6 (a) Description of property	(b) Cost (business use only)	(c) Elected cost
7 Listed property. Enter the amount from line 29	7	

8	Total elected cost of section 179 property. Add amounts in column (c), lines 6 and 7	8	
9	Tentative deduction. Enter the **smaller** of line 5 or line 8	9	
10	Carryover of disallowed deduction from line 13 of your 2009 Form 4562	10	
11	Business income limitation. Enter the smaller of business income (not less than zero) or line 5 (see instructions)	11	
12	Section 179 expense deduction. Add lines 9 and 10, but do not enter more than line 11	12	
13	Carryover of disallowed deduction to 2011. Add lines 9 and 10, less line 12 ▶ 13		

Form 4562 is used when you have purchased items for your business that have an expected life of two or more years. The IRS requires that you track these items, and if they are sold before an item's depreciable life is over, you have to repay any undeserved depreciation that you have taken.

The only part of Form 4562 covered in these instructions is Section 179 deductions. A Section 179 deduction is when you take the entire cost of the item in the year of purchase. Each year a maximum amount is established for businesses using the Section 179 deduction. The maximum amount allowed for 2011 is $500,000.

For 2011 taxes, write $500,000 on **LINE 1**. For any other years check the current IRS Form 4562 instructions for the current figure.

On **LINE 2** write the total you posted to the front of the Q-Equipment envelope.

No one with more than the maximum amount allowed for Section 179 deductions should be preparing their own taxes. Therefore **LINE 3** will be the same as Line 2. If this amount exceeds the current maximum, you are filing Married Filing Separately, or you sell a depreciated or Section 179 item, get guidance from a tax pro.

Everyone else will simply list the items purchased on **LINE 6**, writing the value of the item in both Column (b) and Column (c).

Leave **LINE 7** empty unless you are depreciating your vehicle, then refer to Form 4562 Instructions.

LINE 8 is the Equipment total in Column (c) plus Line 7.

The smaller of Line 5 or Line 8 is written on **LINE 9**.

If you had a carryover of disallowed deductions on last year's return enter that figure on **LINE 10**.

Unless you made more than the Section 179 maximum for that tax year, which will be printed on the tax form, enter your business income from Schedule C Line 7 onto Form 4562 **LINE 11**.

Add Lines 9 and 10 together. If this amount is larger than Line 11, enter that figure on **LINE 12**; otherwise enter the total of Lines 9 and 10.

Subtract Line 12, and enter this amount on **LINE 13**.

If you are depreciating other items, use the IRS instruction book to complete Part II, Part III, Part V and Part VI of Form 4562. Complete these sections before following the instructions for completing the Summary at the bottom of the front of Form 4562.

Part IV	**Summary** (See instructions.)				
21	Listed property. Enter amount from line 28			21	
22	**Total.** Add amounts from line 12, lines 14 through 17, lines 19 and 20 in column (g), and line 21. Enter here and on the appropriate lines of your return. Partnerships and S corporations—see instructions			22	
23	For assets shown above and placed in service during the current year, enter the portion of the basis attributable to section 263A costs	23			

If you completed Part V - Listed Property, transfer the number you put on Line 28 to **LINE 21**, at the bottom of Part IV.

If you did not complete Parts II or III, the figure on LINE 22 will be the total of Line 21 plus Line 12. Otherwise, you will need to add lines 12, 14-17, 19 and 20(g) to Line 21 and put this figure on Line 22.

Unless you are subject to Uniform Capitalization Rules you will enter nothing on LINE 23.

Return to page 62 to learn where to post the number you just put on Line 22 of this form. Then you can continue with the Schedule C instructions.

Taking the Home Office Deduction – Form 8829

Start by filling out the top of IRS Form 8829 – Expenses for Business Use of Your Home. This form can be downloaded at www.IRS.gov, click on the link to Forms and Publications, and look for Form 8829.

A sample copy of the complete IRS Form 8829 appears in Appendix A.

The top portion of Form 8829 begins by asking for the small business owner's name and social security number.

Form **8829**
Department of the Treasury
Internal Revenue Service (99)

Expenses for Business Use of Your Home
▶ File only with Schedule C (Form 1040). Use a separate Form 8829 for each home you used for business during the year.
▶ See separate instructions.

OMB No. 1545-0074
2010
Attachment Sequence No. **176**

Name(s) of proprietor(s) | Your social security number

Part I **Part of Your Home Used for Business**

1	Area used regularly and exclusively for business, regularly for daycare, or for storage of inventory or product samples (see instructions)			1	
2	Total area of home			2	
3	Divide line 1 by line 2. Enter the result as a percentage			3	%
	For daycare facilities not used exclusively for business, go to line 4. All others go to line 7.				
4	Multiply days used for daycare during year by hours used per day	4	hr.		
5	Total hours available for use during the year (365 days x 24 hours) (see instructions)	5	8,760 hr.		
6	Divide line 4 by line 5. Enter the result as a decimal amount	6	.		
7	Business percentage. For daycare facilities not used exclusively for business, multiply line 6 by line 3 (enter the result as a percentage). All others, enter the amount from line 3 ▶			7	%

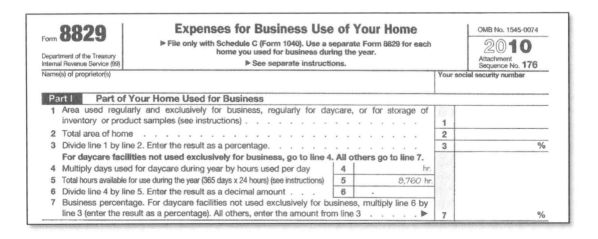

Part I is also where you provide details on the portion of your home used exclusively for your business on a regular basis. Earlier you prepared a page in your notebook titled Home Office Deductions. This information will be entered in Part I of form 8829 as follows.

On **LINE 1** enter the office square footage; the total square footage of your home goes on **LINE 2.** Divide Line 1 by Line 2 to get the percentage of your home set aside for business use, and enter that number on **LINE 3.** You don't need Lines 4-6, they are for daycare facilities. Repeat the number you wrote on Line 3 on **LINE 7.**

Next you will figure the allowable deduction using Part II. The rest of the expenses posted on your Home Office Deductions sheet will be entered here.

Part II — Figure Your Allowable Deduction

8	Enter the amount from Schedule C, line 29, **plus** any net gain or (loss) derived from the business use of your home and shown on Schedule D or Form 4797. If more than one place of business, see instructions			8	
	See instructions for columns (a) and (b) before completing lines 9–21.	(a) Direct expenses	(b) Indirect expenses		
9	Casualty losses (see instructions)	9			
10	Deductible mortgage interest (see instructions)	10			
11	Real estate taxes (see instructions)	11			
12	Add lines 9, 10, and 11	12			
13	Multiply line 12, column (b) by line 7		13		
14	Add line 12, column (a) and line 13			14	
15	Subtract line 14 from line 8. If zero or less, enter -0-			15	
16	Excess mortgage interest (see instructions)	16			
17	Insurance	17			
18	Rent	18			
19	Repairs and maintenance	19			
20	Utilities	20			
21	Other expenses (see instructions)	21			
22	Add lines 16 through 21	22			
23	Multiply line 22, column (b) by line 7		23		
24	Carryover of operating expenses from 2009 Form 8829, line 42		24		
25	Add line 22 column (a), line 23, and line 24			25	
26	Allowable operating expenses. Enter the **smaller** of line 15 or line 25			26	
27	Limit on excess casualty losses and depreciation. Subtract line 26 from line 15			27	
28	Excess casualty losses (see instructions)		28		
29	Depreciation of your home from line 41 below		29		
30	Carryover of excess casualty losses and depreciation from 2009 Form 8829, line 43		30		
31	Add lines 28 through 30			31	
32	Allowable excess casualty losses and depreciation. Enter the **smaller** of line 27 or line 31			32	
33	Add lines 14, 26, and 32			33	
34	Casualty loss portion, if any, from lines 14 and 32. Carry amount to **Form 4684** (see instructions)			34	
35	**Allowable expenses for business use of your home.** Subtract line 34 from line 33. Enter here and on Schedule C, line 30. If your home was used for more than one business, see instructions ▶			35	

Begin by entering the Tentative Profit or Loss from Line 29 of your Schedule C onto **LINE 8** of Form 8829.

Because the amounts you entered in your notebook were for the entire house, all expenses will be entered in the column labeled (b) Indirect Expenses. If you list any expenses on Lines 18-21 that were 100% business, such as a repair to the office ceiling, this will go in column (a) Direct Expenses.

LINE 9 is only filled in if you had casualty losses.

Enter all of the mortgage interest from your 1099 on **LINE 10**.

Real estate taxes paid go on **LINE 11**.

Add Lines 9, 10 and 11 together and put that total on **LINE 12**.

Multiply Line 12 by the % you put on Line 7 of this form, and enter that number on **LINE 13**. Anything leftover will end up on your personal Schedule A.

LINE 14 is the total of Lines 12 and 13.

When you subtract Line 14 from Line 8, and enter that on **LINE 15**, you will know you how much of your mortgage interest and real estate taxes belong on your personal Schedule A.

The rest of your household expenses are reported as follows: Report your insurance on **LINE 17**, rent on **LINE 18**, home repairs and lawn maintenance on **LINE 19**, utilities on **LINE 20**, and any other expenses on **LINE 21**. Post any of these expenses that are 100% business related in Column (a); all others will go in Column (b). Add all of these numbers together, from Column (b), and write the total on **LINE 22**.

Multiply Line 22 x Line 7 and put this on **LINE 23**.

If you have prior year operating carryovers transfer that figure from last year's tax return to **LINE 24**.

Add Column (a) on Line 22, to Lines 23 and 24 and write the total on **LINE 25**.

Compare Line 25 to Line 15 and write the smaller number on **LINE 26**.

Subtract Line 26 from Line 15 and enter that number on **LINE 27**.

If you had casualty losses on Line 9, multiply any losses in excess of the amount listed by the % on Line 7 and enter the results on **LINE 28**.

You will have to complete Parts III and IV of this form before you can fill in the next two lines. Follow the directions below to complete Parts III and IV.

Part III	**Depreciation of Your Home**		
36	Enter the **smaller** of your home's adjusted basis or its fair market value (see instructions)	36	
37	Value of land included on line 36	37	
38	Basis of building. Subtract line 37 from line 36	38	
39	Business basis of building. Multiply line 38 by line 7	39	
40	Depreciation percentage (see instructions)	40	%
41	Depreciation allowable (see instructions). Multiply line 39 by line 40. Enter here and on line 29 above	41	
Part IV	**Carryover of Unallowed Expenses to 2011**		
42	Operating expenses. Subtract line 26 from line 25. If less than zero, enter -0-	42	
43	Excess casualty losses and depreciation. Subtract line 32 from line 31. If less than zero, enter -0-	43	

Depreciation of Your Home requires current basis figures. Your home's basis is the original cost of the home plus all updates made to your home, that have not already been depreciated. Compare your basis to the home's current fair market value and enter the smaller figure on **LINE 36.**

You will find the value assigned to your land on the last property tax statement received. Write that on **LINE 37.**

Subtract Line 37 from Line 36 and enter that on **LINE 38.**

Multiply Line 38 x Line 7 and enter this on **LINE 39.**

If you used your office for the entire year in 2011 write 0.107 on **LINE 40.** If you used it for less than a year, or this is a different tax year, you will need to look up the number for Line 40; it varies based on the first month of use and can be found in the current IRS Form 8829 Instructions at www.IRS.gov.

Multiply Line 7 x Line 40 and write this on **LINE 41.**

Improvements made after the initial year of home office deductions require detailed entries on Form 4562. If you have new improvements, yours is no longer a simple tax return and a visit to a tax professional is advised.

Enter the number you wrote on Line 41 on **LINE 29** in Part II.

You have to fill out Part IV before you can continue; it has only two lines.

To fill in the first box you need to refer to Part II of this form. Subtract Line 26 from Line 25 in Part II, and enter this number on **LINE 42.**

Subtract Line 32 from Line 31 and enter this number on **LINE 43,** unless it is less than zero, then enter zero.

Now you can finish Part II; take the number you wrote on Line 43 and transfer it to **LINE 30.**

Add Lines 28, 29 and 30 and enter the total on **LINE 31.**

Compare Lines 27 and 31; write the smaller figure on **LINE 32.**

Add Lines 14, 26 and 32 and write the sum on **LINE 33.**

If you are required to fill out Form 4684 due to casualty losses you will need to fill in **LINE 34,** otherwise leave it blank.

Subtract Line 34 from Line 33 and enter this number on **LINE 35.** You will also need to enter this figure on your Schedule C tax form, Line 30.

Return to page 64 for instructions on where to enter this figure onto your Schedule C tax return, and follow the rest of the instructions for completing your Schedule C tax form.

Posting Profit or Loss to your 1040 Tax Return

You cannot use tax form 1040EZ or 1040A for your personal taxes when you have Schedule C income; there is nowhere to include business income. You must use Form 1040.

A sample copy of IRS Form 1040 appears in Appendix A. You can download a copy of the current Form 1040 at www.IRS.gov. The portion you are concerned with appears on the following page.

	12	Business income or (loss). Attach Schedule C or C-EZ		12
If you did not get a W-2, see page 20.	13	Capital gain or (loss). Attach Schedule D if required. If not required, check here ▶ ☐		13
	14	Other gains or (losses). Attach Form 4797		14
	15a	IRA distributions . 15a	b Taxable amount . . .	15b
	16a	Pensions and annuities 16a	b Taxable amount . . .	16b
Enclose, but do not attach, any payment. Also, please use **Form 1040-V.**	17	Rental real estate, royalties, partnerships, S corporations, trusts, etc. Attach Schedule E		17
	18	Farm income or (loss). Attach Schedule F		18
	19	Unemployment compensation		19
	20a	Social security benefits 20a	b Taxable amount . . .	20b
	21	Other income. List type and amount		21
	22	Combine the amounts in the far right column for lines 7 through 21. This is your **total income** ▶		22
Adjusted Gross Income	23	Educator expenses	23	
	24	Certain business expenses of reservists, performing artists, and fee-basis government officials. Attach Form 2106 or 2106-EZ	24	
	25	Health savings account deduction. Attach Form 8889 .	25	
	26	Moving expenses. Attach Form 3903	26	
	27	One-half of self-employment tax. Attach Schedule SE .	27	
	28	Self-employed SEP, SIMPLE, and qualified plans . .	28	
	29	Self-employed health insurance deduction	29	
	30	Penalty on early withdrawal of savings	30	
	31a	Alimony paid b Recipient's SSN ▶	31a	
	32	IRA deduction	32	

LINE 12, on the front page of the 1040 is where you post business profit or loss. If you have a loss, your number needs to have a minus in front of it.

When you total all other income sources, on your 1040 personal tax form, an owner who is active in their business will subtract a loss from the total income that gets entered on **LINE 22.**

A Schedule C business loss by an active owner can reduce taxes on other earned income; passive income losses can only be offset by passive gains.

Self Employment Taxes, Self-Employed Health Insurance & Retirement Deposits are all business expenses that are deducted on your personal 1040.

You have already posted your business income or loss to Line 12, but you may have a few more business deductions.

This guide does not explain how to complete your 1040 Personal Tax Return, for information on where to post more business expenses, those deducted on Form 1040, see Other 1040 Deductions on page 75.

If you had net earnings of more than $400 from self-employment, you will need to fill out Schedule SE to figure Self-Employment Taxes before you can finish your 1040. Without it you can't fill in lines 27 and 56.

Calculating Self-Employment Taxes

IRS Schedule SE is used to calculate self employment tax, otherwise known as Social Security and Medicare taxes.

A sample of the complete IRS Schedule SE appears in Appendix A. Download a current form at www.IRS.gov.

Let's start with the top of Schedule SE.

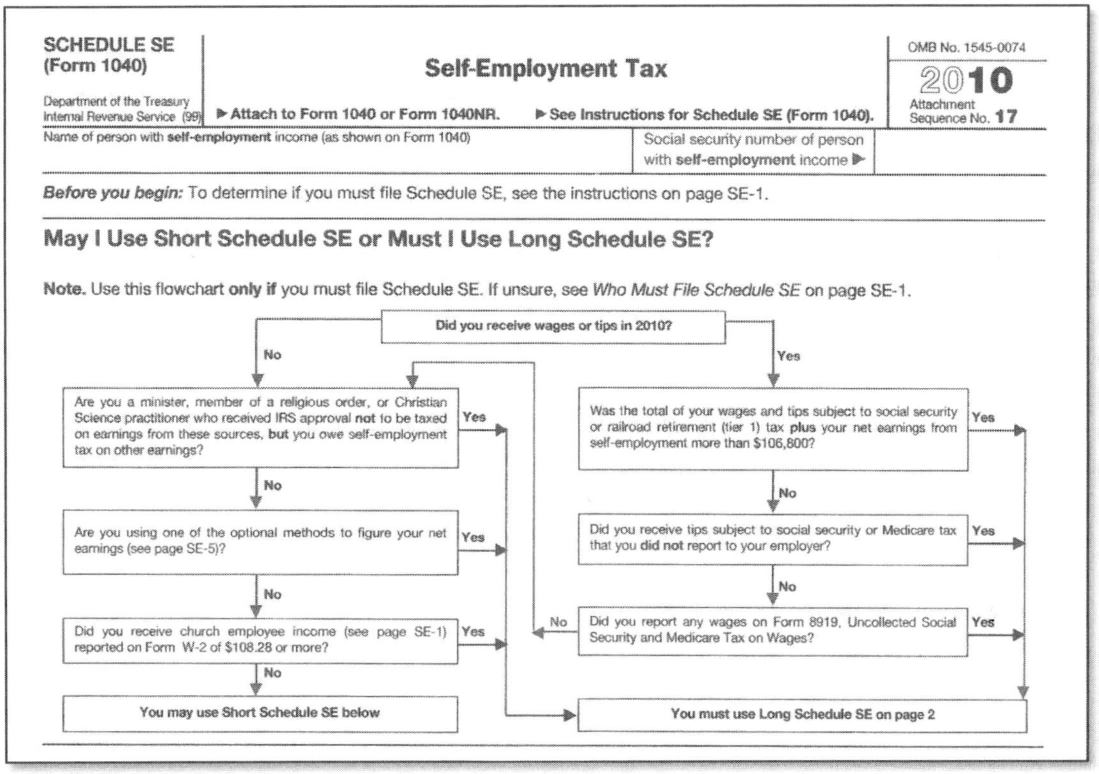
SCHEDULE SE (Form 1040)
Department of the Treasury Internal Revenue Service (99)
Self-Employment Tax
▶ Attach to Form 1040 or Form 1040NR. ▶ See Instructions for Schedule SE (Form 1040).
OMB No. 1545-0074
2010
Attachment Sequence No. 17
Name of person with **self-employment** income (as shown on Form 1040)
Social security number of person with **self-employment** income ▶

Before you begin: To determine if you must file Schedule SE, see the instructions on page SE-1.

May I Use Short Schedule SE or Must I Use Long Schedule SE?

Note. Use this flowchart **only if** you must file Schedule SE. If unsure, see *Who Must File Schedule SE* on page SE-1.

Did you receive wages or tips in 2010?
No
Yes
Are you a minister, member of a religious order, or Christian Science practitioner who received IRS approval not to be taxed on earnings from these sources, but you owe self-employment tax on other earnings?
Yes
No
Are you using one of the optional methods to figure your net earnings (see page SE-5)?
Yes
No
Did you receive church employee income (see page SE-1) reported on Form W-2 of $108.28 or more?
Yes
No
You may use Short Schedule SE below
Was the total of your wages and tips subject to social security or railroad retirement (tier 1) tax plus your net earnings from self-employment more than $106,800?
Yes
No
Did you receive tips subject to social security or Medicare tax that you did not report to your employer?
Yes
No
Did you report any wages on Form 8919, Uncollected Social Security and Medicare Tax on Wages?
No
Yes
You must use Long Schedule SE on page 2

At the very top of the form is a place for the name of the self-employed person and their social security number.

This is followed by a series of questions to help you determine whether or not you need to fill out the back of the form.

Self-employed people with church employee income, and those who want to use the optional method for figuring income, must use the back of this form.

People with total earnings of more than $106,800, unreported tips, or who reported wages on Form 8919 for uncollected Social Security and Medicare Taxes, will also need to complete the back of this form.

Follow the form instructions or get help from a tax professional if you are required to fill out the back of Schedule SE.

Everyone else can skip to the bottom of the front page and answer the six questions found there. The illustration that follows shows the bottom portion of this form so you can follow along

Section A—Short Schedule SE. Caution. Read above to see if you can use Short Schedule SE.

1a	Net farm profit or (loss) from Schedule F, line 36, and farm partnerships, Schedule K-1 (Form 1065), box 14, code A	**1a**	
b	If you received social security retirement or disability benefits, enter the amount of Conservation Reserve Program payments included on Schedule F, line 6b, or listed on Schedule K-1 (Form 1065), box 20, code Y	**1b**	( )
2	Net profit or (loss) from Schedule C, line 31; Schedule C-EZ, line 3; Schedule K-1 (Form 1065), box 14, code A (other than farming); and Schedule K-1 (Form 1065-B), box 9, code J1. Ministers and members of religious orders, see page SE-1 for types of income to report on this line. See page SE-3 for other income to report	**2**	
3	Combine lines 1a, 1b, and 2. Subtract from that total the amount on Form 1040, line 29, or Form 1040NR, line 29, and enter the result (see page SE-3)	**3**	
4	Multiply line 3 by 92.35% (.9235). If less than $400, you do not owe self-employment tax; **do not** file this schedule unless you have an amount on line 1b . . . . ▶	**4**	
	Note. If line 4 is less than $400 due to Conservation Reserve Program payments on line 1b, see page SE-3.		
5	**Self-employment tax.** If the amount on line 4 is: • $106,800 or less, multiply line 4 by 15.3% (.153). Enter the result here and on **Form 1040, line 56,** or **Form 1040NR, line 54** • More than $106,800, multiply line 4 by 2.9% (.029). Then, add $13,243.20 to the result. Enter the total here and on **Form 1040, line 56,** or **Form 1040NR, line 54**	**5**	
6	**Deduction for one-half of self-employment tax.** Multiply line 5 by 50% (.50). Enter the result here and on **Form 1040, line 27,** or **Form 1040NR, line 27** **6**		

LINE 1 is for farmers. Leave it blank.

Post the net profit or loss from Line 31 of your Schedule C to **LINE 2** of your Schedule SE form.

LINE 3 is the total of Lines 1 and 2, minus your self-employee health insurance deduction from Line 29 of your 1040.

Multiply Line 3 by .9235 and enter this on **LINE 4**. If this is less than $400 you do not owe self-employment tax and do not need to file this schedule, unless you have an amount on Line 1b.

If Line 4 is $106,800 or less, multiply this number by .153, and enter the total on **LINE 5**. If it is more than $106,800 multiply the number by .029, add $13,243.20 to the result, and enter on Line 5 instead.

The number on Line 5 must also be entered on **LINE 56 OF YOUR PERSONAL 1040.**

LINE 6 is half of Line 5. That number must also be entered on **LINE 27 OF YOUR PERSONAL 1040.**

That completes the instructions for the self-employment tax form.

A married couple operating a small business together can choose which person's Social Security and Medicare account gets the credit. A married couple can choose to split the business income in any manner they want. Simply complete two Schedule SE forms, one in each name. Combined, the two forms would equal all of the Schedule C profit.

Other 1040 Deductions

Besides lines 12, 27 and 56, where you entered your Schedule C income or loss and Self-Employment Taxes, your 1040 personal tax form has a few other lines where you can take small business deductions.

LINE 28 on your personal 1040 is where a person reports their self-employed personal retirement plan contributions.

Self-employed health insurance expenses are reported on **LINE 29**.

Follow the instructions with your 1040 for these two deductions. Each has its own personal 1040 requirements that may include additional tax forms. You will find rules and instructions for both in the IRS 1040 instruction book, or go online to www.IRS.gov.

There is one other line on your 1040, **LINE 35**, where a small business can enter the domestic production activities deduction. In order to have domestic production your small business would need to have at least one W-2 employee, produce products sold within the US, and fill out a complicated form. If your business is large enough to benefit from this deduction you need to see a tax professional for help based on your industry.

Finishing the Job

You are now ready to complete the rest of your personal 1040 tax return using the IRS 1040 Instruction Book. Fill it out just like you did in years prior to operating a business, adding business income and deductions as instructed. If having a small business makes it too confusing, take it all to a tax professional.

Anyone expecting to owe $1,000 or more in taxes for the following year is required to make estimated payments. These payments are based on the current year's taxable income and also referred to as Quarterly Tax Payments. As long as you pay in at least 100% of the taxes owed in the prior year, during the current tax year, you won't get hit with a penalty, based on current laws.

Postmark your return by April 15th and get a receipt when you put it in the mail.

The next chapter in this book will explain what to do with all of the papers you've collected. They're crucial to surviving an IRS tax audit.

DEVELOPING AN AUDIT-PROOF MINDSET

Establishing an audit-proof mindset is simple. When all income and expenses for a business are kept separate from personal funds, and every income and expense has a paper trail, and you almost always survive an audit.

The exception comes when you have misinterpreted tax law. That's where the tax professional can help. If you're doing your own taxes, visiting a good tax accountant 2-3 times a decade, or any time life or business circumstances change, will keep you informed on current laws and help you to pay less tax.

Tax Pro Rule #10

Without receipts, you will fail an audit.

Box or bag your tax receipts, and

keep those records for at least 6 years.

Copies of tax returns should be kept

a minimum of 10 years.

Storage of tax records doesn't have to be fancy. Simply use a 1-2 gallon plastic food storage bag. Put the entire year's worth of records inside, write the tax year on the bag in indelible ink, and place that bag into a cardboard file box.

If you have lots of receipts, you can store each year in a shoebox labeled with the tax year.

Label a big storage box Tax Receipts; this box needs to be large enough to hold 6-10 giant Ziploc bags, or shoeboxes, each filled with a year's worth of receipts. When the storage box is full, file it away and start another, or if those records are older than 6 years, remove and shred the oldest to make room for the current year.

Don't put you're the copy of your tax return or W-2's into this box. You will need a copy of your tax return and its accompanying W-2's if you apply for a mortgage or loan, so store then in a more convenient place. Keeping them easily accessible will make filling out those applications easier, and you'll have all of the tax papers the bank will require handy.

The tax notebook you prepared will be useful too, so don't hide it away in the box. Those numbers can be useful when writing a business plan or making inventory projections. Store it with your other business financial information.

An IRS audit may sound scary, but an audit is nothing more than a meeting where the taxpayer is expected to show receipts that back up the numbers he or she put onto a particular year's tax return. The person who has receipts is done quickly.

But, because individuals are extremely likely to say too much during an audit, exposing other issues and causing the IRS to ask for more meetings and more receipts, it's always smart to hire a tax accountant or tax company that specializes in audits to attend that meeting for you.

If you have a regular tax professional call them the day you receive the audit letter; dealing with audits on the returns that they prepared is part of a tax professional's service. And, they can represent you for any other audits, including those on tax returns that you prepared yourself.

Take your bag of receipt envelopes for the year being audited with you when you meet with your tax professional. He or she will know which papers will be necessary to win the audit; and if you've followed all of the Tax Pro Rules, those receipts will be in that bag, and easy to find.

Planning for the Future

Many independent business people never move beyond the ***Annual Tax Mess Organizer's*** method of dealing with the annual chore of preparing information for their tax return. It may work well for the business owner with a small stack of expense receipts or self-employed people who hate doing paperwork, since they only have to tackle the job once a year.

But, if you want to learn how to use that same financial information to increase your profits you might want to try ***30 Minutes to a Better Business: A Monthly Financial Organizer for the Self-Employed*** next year. It can be used monthly, quarterly, or semi-annually to track your business income and expenses and uses the same simple method taught in the Annual Tax Mess Organizer. This book includes all of the forms necessary for posting your income and expenses monthly, tracking new and old inventory, and creating your annual tax report. Plus, it teaches you how to use that information to improve your bottom line.

However, if you don't prepare your own tax return, **Do My Business Taxes Please: A Financial Organizer for Self-Employed Individuals & Their Tax Preparers** may be the right choice for future tax years. It too includes all of the forms you will need to post your income and expenses on a regular basis, track inventory properly, and create an annual tax report. This book also teaches you what you need to do before seeing your tax professional if you want to pay less tax and keep your business audit proof.

No matter which book you use next year, you'll have all of the information necessary to prepare an accurate tax return, and be ready to win a tax audit, should one arise.

If you have inventory on your shelves at the close of the current tax year, you are going to need a Prior Year Inventory Report to track end of year inventory for next year's tax return. And, if you will be adding new inventory you'll also need a New Inventory Report. Now is the time to start both.

If you are not purchasing one of the two recommended organizers, with pre-printed forms, you will need to prepare a fresh spiral notebook for the next tax year. Write the new tax year on the front of that notebook, and create those two inventory reports now, while you've got this book open; remember to leave blank pages for additional report pages.

Keep your new notebook, or the new organizer you have purchased, where you normally receive new inventory. This will make it easy to record new inventory the moment it arrives. Starting your organizer now will give you a big jump on next year's tax mess.

TAX PROFESSIONALS

Tax professionals provide help with tax returns all across the United States, but not all are qualified to do more than fill out a simple 1040 personal tax return.

When selecting a new tax preparer never choose one based on his or her reputation for getting everyone huge refunds. Everyone's tax circumstances are different, even when they appear to be the same to a person who has no tax training. And, a lot of large tax refunds would never survive a thorough IRS audit.

Before allowing someone to do your taxes, ask how many small business tax returns they have prepared. If they have done less than 50 Schedule C returns go elsewhere; many seasonal tax offices allow first year preparers to do small business returns. Although this may be good training for the new preparer, it's a bad deal for you. Experience is what makes a tax professional good.

The federal government is currently instituting a licensing system for tax preparers; prior to that only two states required proof that preparers were qualified to prepare personal tax returns. California and Oregon have tested and licensed their preparers for decades; most states have no educational requirements for tax preparers.

Always ask about a tax preparer's experience and licenses before hiring them to do your taxes. All accountants are licensed, but you want a tax accountant, someone who specializes in small business tax returns. Accountants know more about tax law than most seasonal preparers. However, a licensed tax preparer who specializes in Schedule C tax returns will often know just as much about small business tax returns.

Choose an accountant or tax professional who does tax returns for others in your line of business, and choose one that fits your budget. Get someone who teaches you how to pay less tax legally, and never hire someone who suggests you break the rules.

Here's a quick recap of those ten tax pro rules.

Tax Pro Rule #1

Absolutely all business income, including all cash & tips, must be deposited into a separate checking account used only for business funds.

Tax Pro Rule #2

Every penny spent or charged for your business needs a paper trail. If a receipt is not provided, you can make your own; just include all of the necessary details.

Tax Pro Rule #3

Every business barter exchange requires a paper trail assigning value to your time, or the product you traded for another's time or product.

Tax Pro Rule #4

Sorting expense receipts is as easy as ABC, when you use the business expense alphabet.

Tax Pro Rule #5

Any equipment purchased, with an expected life of two or more years must be depreciated or expensed as a Section 179 deduction.

Tax Pro Rule #6

Unless you have a vehicle used only for business, keep a notebook in the car and write down every business mile.

Tax Pro Rule #7

All items purchased or created for resale, are considered inventory by the IRS. Inventory expenses can only be deducted as that inventory is sold.

Tax Pro Rule #8

No matter how good your tax professional is, if you don't provide all of the necessary information and figures, your tax return will be wrong.

Tax Pro Rule #9

Tax laws change every year, sometimes offering huge tax savings for only a short time. Even if you do your own taxes, it is wise to speak with a tax pro occasionally, just to keep up on new tax credits and tax planning opportunities.

Tax Pro Rule #10

Without receipts, you will fail an audit. Box or bag your tax receipts, and keep those records for at least 6 years. Copies of tax returns should be kept a minimum of 10 years.

APPENDIX A – TAX FORMS

The following IRS forms represent those used during the 2010 tax season. They are printed here so that you can become familiar with their format. These are the same forms addressed in the chapter on preparing your own Schedule C tax return.

Although many IRS tax forms remain the same for years, the year at the top always changes. You can download forms for any recent tax year at www.IRS.gov . If you are preparing a prior year tax return you will need to download forms and instructions for that particular tax year.

Current year tax booklets and forms are generally available in post office lobbies all across the United States during tax season.

The following IRS tax forms appear in this section:

- Schedule C – Profit or Loss From Business
- Schedule SE – Self-Employment Tax
- Form 4562 – Depreciation and Amortization
- Form 8829 – Expenses for Business Use of Your Home
- Form 1040 – U.S. Individual Income Tax Return

SCHEDULE C (Form 1040)

Department of the Treasury Internal Revenue Service (99)

Profit or Loss From Business

(Sole Proprietorship)

▶ **Partnerships, joint ventures, etc., generally must file Form 1065 or 1065-B.**
▶ **Attach to Form 1040, 1040NR, or 1041.** ▶ **See Instructions for Schedule C (Form 1040).**

OMB No. 1545-0074

2010

Attachment Sequence No. **09**

Name of proprietor | **Social security number (SSN)**

A Principal business or profession, including product or service (see instructions) | **B Enter code from pages C-9, 10, & 11** ▶

C Business name. If no separate business name, leave blank. | **D Employer ID number (EIN), if any**

E Business address (including suite or room no.) ▶
City, town or post office, state, and ZIP code

F Accounting method: **(1)** ☐ Cash **(2)** ☐ Accrual **(3)** ☐ Other (specify) ▶

G Did you "materially participate" in the operation of this business during 2010? If "No," see instructions for limit on losses ☐ **Yes** ☐ **No**

H If you started or acquired this business during 2010, check here ▶ ☐

Part I Income

1	**Gross receipts or sales. Caution.** See instructions and check the box if: • This income was reported to you on Form W-2 and the "Statutory employee" box on that form was checked, or • You are a member of a qualified joint venture reporting only rental real estate income not subject to self-employment tax. Also see instructions for limit on losses. ▶ ☐	1	
2	Returns and allowances	2	
3	Subtract line 2 from line 1	3	
4	Cost of goods sold (from line 42 on page 2)	4	
5	**Gross profit.** Subtract line 4 from line 3	5	
6	Other income, including federal and state gasoline or fuel tax credit or refund (see instructions)	6	
7	**Gross income.** Add lines 5 and 6 ▶	7	

Part II Expenses. Enter expenses for business use of your home **only** on line 30.

8	Advertising	8		18	Office expense	18	
9	Car and truck expenses (see instructions)	9		19	Pension and profit-sharing plans	19	
10	Commissions and fees	10		20	Rent or lease (see instructions):		
11	Contract labor (see instructions)	11		a	Vehicles, machinery, and equipment	20a	
12	Depletion	12		b	Other business property	20b	
13	Depreciation and section 179 expense deduction (not included in Part III) (see instructions)	13		21	Repairs and maintenance	21	
				22	Supplies (not included in Part III)	22	
				23	Taxes and licenses	23	
				24	Travel, meals, and entertainment:		
				a	Travel	24a	
14	Employee benefit programs (other than on line 19)	14		b	Deductible meals and entertainment (see instructions)	24b	
15	Insurance (other than health)	15		25	Utilities	25	
16	Interest:			26	Wages (less employment credits)	26	
a	Mortgage (paid to banks, etc.)	16a		27	Other expenses (from line 48 on page 2)	27	
b	Other	16b					
17	Legal and professional services	17					

28	**Total expenses** before expenses for business use of home. Add lines 8 through 27 ▶	28	
29	Tentative profit or (loss). Subtract line 28 from line 7	29	
30	Expenses for business use of your home. Attach **Form 8829**	30	
31	**Net profit or (loss).** Subtract line 30 from line 29. • If a profit, enter on both **Form 1040, line 12,** and **Schedule SE, line 2,** or on **Form 1040NR, line 13** (if you checked the box on line 1, see instructions). Estates and trusts, enter on **Form 1041, line 3.** • If a loss, you **must** go to line 32.	31	

32 If you have a loss, check the box that describes your investment in this activity (see instructions).
• If you checked 32a, enter the loss on both **Form 1040, line 12,** and **Schedule SE, line 2,** or on **Form 1040NR, line 13** (if you checked the box on line 1, see the line 31 instructions). Estates and trusts, enter on **Form 1041, line 3.**
• If you checked 32b, you **must** attach **Form 6198.** Your loss may be limited.

32a ☐ All investment is at risk.
32b ☐ Some investment is not at risk.

For Paperwork Reduction Act Notice, see your tax return instructions. Cat. No. 11334P **Schedule C (Form 1040) 2010**

Schedule C (Form 1040) 2010 Page **2**

Part III **Cost of Goods Sold** (see instructions)

33 Method(s) used to value closing inventory: a ☐ Cost b ☐ Lower of cost or market c ☐ Other (attach explanation)

34 Was there any change in determining quantities, costs, or valuations between opening and closing inventory? If "Yes," attach explanation . . . ☐ Yes ☐ No

35	Inventory at beginning of year. If different from last year's closing inventory, attach explanation	35	
36	Purchases less cost of items withdrawn for personal use	36	
37	Cost of labor. Do not include any amounts paid to yourself	37	
38	Materials and supplies	38	
39	Other costs	39	
40	Add lines 35 through 39	40	
41	Inventory at end of year	41	
42	**Cost of goods sold.** Subtract line 41 from line 40. Enter the result here and on page 1, line 4	42	

Part IV **Information on Your Vehicle.** Complete this part **only** if you are claiming car or truck expenses on line 9 and are not required to file Form 4562 for this business. See the instructions for line 13 to find out if you must file Form 4562.

43 When did you place your vehicle in service for business purposes? (month, day, year) ▶ ____ / ____ / ____

44 Of the total number of miles you drove your vehicle during 2010, enter the number of miles you used your vehicle for:

a Business ________ b Commuting (see instructions) ________ c Other ________

45 Was your vehicle available for personal use during off-duty hours? . . . ☐ Yes ☐ No

46 Do you (or your spouse) have another vehicle available for personal use? . . . ☐ Yes ☐ No

47a Do you have evidence to support your deduction? . . . ☐ Yes ☐ No

b If "Yes," is the evidence written? . . . ☐ Yes ☐ No

Part V **Other Expenses.** List below business expenses not included on lines 8–26 or line 30.

48 Total other expenses. Enter here and on page 1, line 27	48	

Schedule C (Form 1040) 2010

SCHEDULE SE (Form 1040)

Department of the Treasury Internal Revenue Service (99)

Self-Employment Tax

▶ Attach to Form 1040 or Form 1040NR. ▶ See Instructions for Schedule SE (Form 1040).

OMB No. 1545-0074

2010

Attachment Sequence No. **17**

Name of person with **self-employment** income (as shown on Form 1040)	Social security number of person with **self-employment** income ▶

Before you begin: To determine if you must file Schedule SE, see the instructions on page SE-1.

May I Use Short Schedule SE or Must I Use Long Schedule SE?

Note. Use this flowchart **only if** you must file Schedule SE. If unsure, see *Who Must File Schedule SE* on page SE-1.

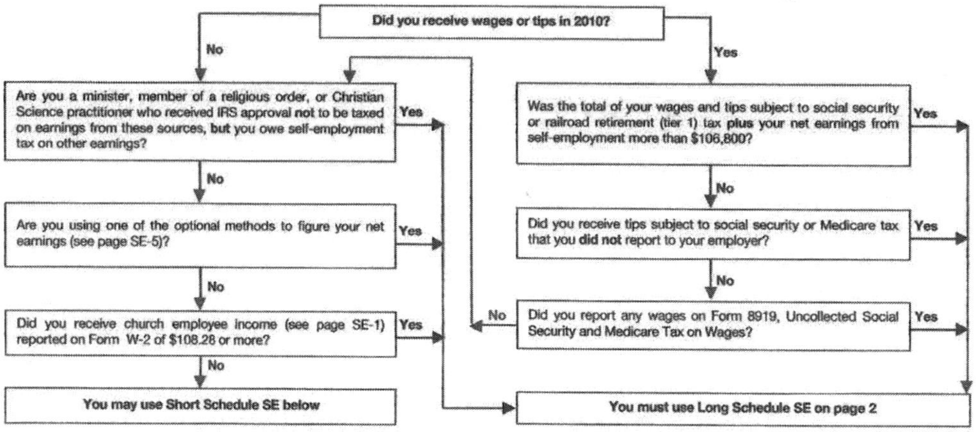
Did you receive wages or tips in 2010?
No
Yes
Are you a minister, member of a religious order, or Christian Science practitioner who received IRS approval not to be taxed on earnings from these sources, but you owe self-employment tax on other earnings?
Yes
No
Are you using one of the optional methods to figure your net earnings (see page SE-5)?
Yes
No
Did you receive church employee income (see page SE-1) reported on Form W-2 of $108.28 or more?
Yes
No
You may use Short Schedule SE below
Was the total of your wages and tips subject to social security or railroad retirement (tier 1) tax plus your net earnings from self-employment more than $106,800?
Yes
No
Did you receive tips subject to social security or Medicare tax that you did not report to your employer?
Yes
No
Did you report any wages on Form 8919, Uncollected Social Security and Medicare Tax on Wages?
No
Yes
You must use Long Schedule SE on page 2

Section A—Short Schedule SE. Caution. Read above to see if you can use Short Schedule SE.

1a	Net farm profit or (loss) from Schedule F, line 36, and farm partnerships, Schedule K-1 (Form 1065), box 14, code A	**1a**	
b	If you received social security retirement or disability benefits, enter the amount of Conservation Reserve Program payments included on Schedule F, line 6b, or listed on Schedule K-1 (Form 1065), box 20, code Y	**1b**	( )
2	Net profit or (loss) from Schedule C, line 31; Schedule C-EZ, line 3; Schedule K-1 (Form 1065), box 14, code A (other than farming); and Schedule K-1 (Form 1065-B), box 9, code J1. Ministers and members of religious orders, see page SE-1 for types of income to report on this line. See page SE-3 for other income to report	**2**	
3	Combine lines 1a, 1b, and 2. Subtract from that total the amount on Form 1040, line 29, or Form 1040NR, line 29, and enter the result (see page SE-3)	**3**	
4	Multiply line 3 by 92.35% (.9235). If less than $400, you do not owe self-employment tax; **do not** file this schedule unless you have an amount on line 1b . . . . ▶	**4**	
	Note. If line 4 is less than $400 due to Conservation Reserve Program payments on line 1b, see page SE-3.		
5	**Self-employment tax.** If the amount on line 4 is: • $106,800 or less, multiply line 4 by 15.3% (.153). Enter the result here and on **Form 1040, line 56,** or **Form 1040NR, line 54** • More than $106,800, multiply line 4 by 2.9% (.029). Then, add $13,243.20 to the result. Enter the total here and on **Form 1040, line 56,** or **Form 1040NR, line 54**	**5**	
6	**Deduction for one-half of self-employment tax.** Multiply line 5 by 50% (.50). Enter the result here and on **Form 1040, line 27,** or **Form 1040NR, line 27** **6**		

For Paperwork Reduction Act Notice, see your tax return instructions. Cat. No. 11358Z **Schedule SE (Form 1040) 2010**

Schedule SE (Form 1040) 2010 | Attachment Sequence No. **17** | Page **2**

Name of person with **self-employment** income (as shown on Form 1040)	Social security number of person with **self-employment** income ▶	

Section B—Long Schedule SE

Part I Self-Employment Tax

Note. If your only income subject to self-employment tax is **church employee income,** see page SE-3 for specific instructions. Also see page SE-1 for the definition of church employee income.

A	If you are a minister, member of a religious order, or Christian Science practitioner **and** you filed Form 4361, but you had $400 or more of **other** net earnings from self-employment, check here and continue with Part I . . . . ▶ ☐			
1a	Net farm profit or (loss) from Schedule F, line 36, and farm partnerships, Schedule K-1 (Form 1065), box 14, code A. **Note.** Skip lines 1a and 1b if you use the farm optional method (see page SE-5)	1a		
b	If you received social security retirement or disability benefits, enter the amount of Conservation Reserve Program payments included on Schedule F, line 6b, or listed on Schedule K-1 (Form 1065), box 20, code Y	1b	(	)
2	Net profit or (loss) from Schedule C, line 31; Schedule C-EZ, line 3; Schedule K-1 (Form 1065), box 14, code A (other than farming); and Schedule K-1 (Form 1065-B), box 9, code J1. Ministers and members of religious orders, see page SE-1 for types of income to report on this line. See page SE-4 for other income to report. **Note.** Skip this line if you use the nonfarm optional method (see page SE-5)	2		
3	Combine lines 1a, 1b, and 2. Subtract from that total the amount on Form 1040, line 29, or Form 1040NR, line 29, and enter the result (see page SE-3)	3		
4a	If line 3 is more than zero, multiply line 3 by 92.35% (.9235). Otherwise, enter amount from line 3. **Note.** If line 4a is less than $400 due to Conservation Reserve Program payments on line 1b, see page SE-3.	4a		
b	If you elect one or both of the optional methods, enter the total of lines 15 and 17 here . .	4b		
c	Combine lines 4a and 4b. If less than $400, **stop**; you do not owe self-employment tax. **Exception.** If less than $400 and you had **church employee income,** enter -0- and continue ▶	4c		
5a	Enter your **church employee income** from Form W-2. See page SE-1 for definition of church employee income **5a**			
b	Multiply line 5a by 92.35% (.9235). If less than $100, enter -0-	5b		
6	Add lines 4c and 5b	6		
7	Maximum amount of combined wages and self-employment earnings subject to social security tax or the 6.2% portion of the 7.65% railroad retirement (tier 1) tax for 2010	7	106,800	00
8a	Total social security wages and tips (total of boxes 3 and 7 on Form(s) W-2) and railroad retirement (tier 1) compensation. If $106,800 or more, skip lines 8b through 10, and go to line 11 **8a**			
b	Unreported tips subject to social security tax (from Form 4137, line 10) **8b**			
c	Wages subject to social security tax (from Form 8919, line 10) **8c**			
d	Add lines 8a, 8b, and 8c	8d		
9	Subtract line 8d from line 7. If zero or less, enter -0- here and on line 10 and go to line 11 . ▶	9		
10	Multiply the **smaller** of line 6 or line 9 by 12.4% (.124)	10		
11	Multiply line 6 by 2.9% (.029)	11		
12	**Self-employment tax.** Add lines 10 and 11. Enter here and on **Form 1040, line 56,** or **Form 1040NR, line 54**	12		
13	**Deduction for one-half of self-employment tax.** Multiply line 12 by 50% (.50). Enter the result here and on **Form 1040, line 27, or Form 1040NR, line 27** . **13**			

Part II Optional Methods To Figure Net Earnings (see page SE-4)

Farm Optional Method. You may use this method **only** if **(a)** your gross farm income[1] was not more than $6,720, **or (b)** your net farm profits[2] were less than $4,851.

14	Maximum income for optional methods	14	4,480	00
15	Enter the **smaller** of: two-thirds (2/3) of gross farm income[1] (not less than zero) **or** $4,480. Also include this amount on line 4b above	15		

Nonfarm Optional Method. You may use this method **only** if **(a)** your net nonfarm profits[3] were less than $4,851 and also less than 72.189% of your gross nonfarm income,[4] **and (b)** you had net earnings from self-employment of at least $400 in 2 of the prior 3 years. **Caution.** You may use this method no more than five times.

16	Subtract line 15 from line 14	16		
17	Enter the **smaller** of: two-thirds (2/3) of gross nonfarm income[4] (not less than zero) **or** the amount on line 16. Also include this amount on line 4b above	17		

[1] From Sch. F, line 11, and Sch. K-1 (Form 1065), box 14, code B.

[2] From Sch. F, line 36, and Sch. K-1 (Form 1065), box 14, code A—minus the amount you would have entered on line 1b had you not used the optional method.

[3] From Sch. C, line 31; Sch. C-EZ, line 3; Sch. K-1 (Form 1065), box 14, code A; and Sch. K-1 (Form 1065-B), box 9, code J1.

[4] From Sch. C, line 7; Sch. C-EZ, line 1; Sch. K-1 (Form 1065), box 14, code C; and Sch. K-1 (Form 1065-B), box 9, code J2.

Schedule SE (Form 1040) 2010

Form **4562**

Department of the Treasury
Internal Revenue Service (99)

Depreciation and Amortization
(Including Information on Listed Property)

▶ See separate instructions. ▶ Attach to your tax return.

OMB No. 1545-0172

2010

Attachment Sequence No. **67**

Name(s) shown on return	Business or activity to which this form relates	Identifying number

Part I **Election To Expense Certain Property Under Section 179**
Note: *If you have any listed property, complete Part V before you complete Part I.*

1	Maximum amount (see instructions)	1	
2	Total cost of section 179 property placed in service (see instructions)	2	
3	Threshold cost of section 179 property before reduction in limitation (see instructions)	3	
4	Reduction in limitation. Subtract line 3 from line 2. If zero or less, enter -0-	4	
5	Dollar limitation for tax year. Subtract line 4 from line 1. If zero or less, enter -0-. If married filing separately, see instructions	5	

6	(a) Description of property	(b) Cost (business use only)	(c) Elected cost

7	Listed property. Enter the amount from line 29	7	
8	Total elected cost of section 179 property. Add amounts in column (c), lines 6 and 7	8	
9	Tentative deduction. Enter the **smaller** of line 5 or line 8	9	
10	Carryover of disallowed deduction from line 13 of your 2009 Form 4562	10	
11	Business income limitation. Enter the smaller of business income (not less than zero) or line 5 (see instructions)	11	
12	Section 179 expense deduction. Add lines 9 and 10, but do not enter more than line 11	12	
13	Carryover of disallowed deduction to 2011. Add lines 9 and 10, less line 12 ▶	13	

Note: *Do not use Part II or Part III below for listed property. Instead, use Part V.*

Part II **Special Depreciation Allowance and Other Depreciation (Do not** include listed property.) (See instructions.)

14	Special depreciation allowance for qualified property (other than listed property) placed in service during the tax year (see instructions)	14	
15	Property subject to section 168(f)(1) election	15	
16	Other depreciation (including ACRS)	16	

Part III **MACRS Depreciation (Do not** include listed property.) (See instructions.)

Section A

17	MACRS deductions for assets placed in service in tax years beginning before 2010	17	
18	If you are electing to group any assets placed in service during the tax year into one or more general asset accounts, check here ▶ ☐		

Section B—Assets Placed in Service During 2010 Tax Year Using the General Depreciation System

(a) Classification of property	(b) Month and year placed in service	(c) Basis for depreciation (business/investment use only—see instructions)	(d) Recovery period	(e) Convention	(f) Method	(g) Depreciation deduction
19a 3-year property						
b 5-year property						
c 7-year property						
d 10-year property						
e 15-year property						
f 20-year property						
g 25-year property			25 yrs.		S/L	
h Residential rental property			27.5 yrs.	MM	S/L	
			27.5 yrs.	MM	S/L	
i Nonresidential real property			39 yrs.	MM	S/L	
				MM	S/L	

Section C—Assets Placed in Service During 2010 Tax Year Using the Alternative Depreciation System

(a) Classification of property	(b)	(c)	(d)	(e)	(f)	(g)
20a Class life					S/L	
b 12-year			12 yrs.		S/L	
c 40-year			40 yrs.	MM	S/L	

Part IV **Summary** (See instructions.)

21	Listed property. Enter amount from line 28	21	
22	**Total.** Add amounts from line 12, lines 14 through 17, lines 19 and 20 in column (g), and line 21. Enter here and on the appropriate lines of your return. Partnerships and S corporations—see instructions	22	
23	For assets shown above and placed in service during the current year, enter the portion of the basis attributable to section 263A costs	23	

For Paperwork Reduction Act Notice, see separate instructions. Cat. No. 12906N Form **4562** (2010)

Form 4562 (2010) Page 2

Part V Listed Property (Include automobiles, certain other vehicles, certain computers, and property used for entertainment, recreation, or amusement.)

Note: *For any vehicle for which you are using the standard mileage rate or deducting lease expense, complete **only** 24a, 24b, columns (a) through (c) of Section A, all of Section B, and Section C if applicable.*

Section A—Depreciation and Other Information (Caution: *See the instructions for limits for passenger automobiles.)*

24a Do you have evidence to support the business/investment use claimed? ☐ Yes ☐ No **24b** If "Yes," is the evidence written? ☐ Yes ☐ No

(a) Type of property (list vehicles first)	(b) Date placed in service	(c) Business/ investment use percentage	(d) Cost or other basis	(e) Basis for depreciation (business/investment use only)	(f) Recovery period	(g) Method/ Convention	(h) Depreciation deduction	(i) Elected section 179 cost
25 Special depreciation allowance for qualified listed property placed in service during the tax year and used more than 50% in a qualified business use (see instructions) .						25		
26 Property used more than 50% in a qualified business use:								
		%						
		%						
		%						
27 Property used 50% or less in a qualified business use:								
		%				S/L –		
		%				S/L –		
		%				S/L –		
28 Add amounts in column (h), lines 25 through 27. Enter here and on line 21, page 1 .						28		
29 Add amounts in column (i), line 26. Enter here and on line 7, page 1							29	

Section B—Information on Use of Vehicles

Complete this section for vehicles used by a sole proprietor, partner, or other "more than 5% owner," or related person. If you provided vehicles to your employees, first answer the questions in Section C to see if you meet an exception to completing this section for those vehicles.

	(a) Vehicle 1		(b) Vehicle 2		(c) Vehicle 3		(d) Vehicle 4		(e) Vehicle 5		(f) Vehicle 6	
30 Total business/investment miles driven during the year (**do not** include commuting miles) .												
31 Total commuting miles driven during the year												
32 Total other personal (noncommuting) miles driven												
33 Total miles driven during the year. Add lines 30 through 32												
	Yes	No	Yes	No	Yes	No	Yes	No	Yes	No	Yes	No
34 Was the vehicle available for personal use during off-duty hours?												
35 Was the vehicle used primarily by a more than 5% owner or related person? . . .												
36 Is another vehicle available for personal use?												

Section C—Questions for Employers Who Provide Vehicles for Use by Their Employees

Answer these questions to determine if you meet an exception to completing Section B for vehicles used by employees who **are not** more than 5% owners or related persons (see instructions).

	Yes	No
37 Do you maintain a written policy statement that prohibits all personal use of vehicles, including commuting, by your employees?		
38 Do you maintain a written policy statement that prohibits personal use of vehicles, except commuting, by your employees? See the instructions for vehicles used by corporate officers, directors, or 1% or more owners		
39 Do you treat all use of vehicles by employees as personal use?		
40 Do you provide more than five vehicles to your employees, obtain information from your employees about the use of the vehicles, and retain the information received?		
41 Do you meet the requirements concerning qualified automobile demonstration use? (See instructions.) . . .		

Note: *If your answer to 37, 38, 39, 40, or 41 is "Yes," do not complete Section B for the covered vehicles.*

Part VI Amortization

(a) Description of costs	(b) Date amortization begins	(c) Amortizable amount	(d) Code section	(e) Amortization period or percentage	(f) Amortization for this year
42 Amortization of costs that begins during your 2010 tax year (see instructions):					
43 Amortization of costs that began before your 2010 tax year				43	
44 **Total.** Add amounts in column (f). See the instructions for where to report				44	

Form **4562** (2010)

[Form 8829 has only one side]

Form **8829**

Department of the Treasury
Internal Revenue Service (99)

Expenses for Business Use of Your Home

▶ File only with Schedule C (Form 1040). Use a separate Form 8829 for each home you used for business during the year.

▶ See separate instructions.

OMB No. 1545-0074

2010

Attachment Sequence No. **176**

Name(s) of proprietor(s) | Your social security number

Part I Part of Your Home Used for Business

1	Area used regularly and exclusively for business, regularly for daycare, or for storage of inventory or product samples (see instructions)	1	
2	Total area of home	2	
3	Divide line 1 by line 2. Enter the result as a percentage	3	%
	For daycare facilities not used exclusively for business, go to line 4. All others go to line 7.		
4	Multiply days used for daycare during year by hours used per day — 4: hr.		
5	Total hours available for use during the year (365 days x 24 hours) (see instructions) — 5: 8,760 hr.		
6	Divide line 4 by line 5. Enter the result as a decimal amount — 6: .		
7	Business percentage. For daycare facilities not used exclusively for business, multiply line 6 by line 3 (enter the result as a percentage). All others, enter the amount from line 3 ▶	7	%

Part II Figure Your Allowable Deduction

			(a) Direct expenses	(b) Indirect expenses		
8	Enter the amount from Schedule C, line 29, **plus** any net gain or (loss) derived from the business use of your home and shown on Schedule D or Form 4797. If more than one place of business, see instructions				8	
	See instructions for columns (a) and (b) before completing lines 9-21.					
9	Casualty losses (see instructions)	9				
10	Deductible mortgage interest (see instructions)	10				
11	Real estate taxes (see instructions)	11				
12	Add lines 9, 10, and 11	12				
13	Multiply line 12, column (b) by line 7		13			
14	Add line 12, column (a) and line 13				14	
15	Subtract line 14 from line 8. If zero or less, enter -0-				15	
16	Excess mortgage interest (see instructions)	16				
17	Insurance	17				
18	Rent	18				
19	Repairs and maintenance	19				
20	Utilities	20				
21	Other expenses (see instructions)	21				
22	Add lines 16 through 21	22				
23	Multiply line 22, column (b) by line 7		23			
24	Carryover of operating expenses from 2009 Form 8829, line 42		24			
25	Add line 22 column (a), line 23, and line 24				25	
26	Allowable operating expenses. Enter the **smaller** of line 15 or line 25				26	
27	Limit on excess casualty losses and depreciation. Subtract line 26 from line 15				27	
28	Excess casualty losses (see instructions)		28			
29	Depreciation of your home from line 41 below		29			
30	Carryover of excess casualty losses and depreciation from 2009 Form 8829, line 43		30			
31	Add lines 28 through 30				31	
32	Allowable excess casualty losses and depreciation. Enter the **smaller** of line 27 or line 31				32	
33	Add lines 14, 26, and 32				33	
34	Casualty loss portion, if any, from lines 14 and 32. Carry amount to **Form 4684** (see instructions)				34	
35	**Allowable expenses for business use of your home.** Subtract line 34 from line 33. Enter here and on Schedule C, line 30. If your home was used for more than one business, see instructions ▶				35	

Part III Depreciation of Your Home

36	Enter the **smaller** of your home's adjusted basis or its fair market value (see instructions)	36	
37	Value of land included on line 36	37	
38	Basis of building. Subtract line 37 from line 36	38	
39	Business basis of building. Multiply line 38 by line 7	39	
40	Depreciation percentage (see instructions)	40	%
41	Depreciation allowable (see instructions). Multiply line 39 by line 40. Enter here and on line 29 above	41	

Part IV Carryover of Unallowed Expenses to 2011

42	Operating expenses. Subtract line 26 from line 25. If less than zero, enter -0-	42	
43	Excess casualty losses and depreciation. Subtract line 32 from line 31. If less than zero, enter -0-	43	

For Paperwork Reduction Act Notice, see your tax return instructions. Cat. No. 13232M Form **8829** (2010)

Form **1040** Department of the Treasury—Internal Revenue Service
U.S. Individual Income Tax Return 2010 (99) IRS Use Only—Do not write or staple in this space.

Name, Address, and SSN

See separate instructions.

PRINT CLEARLY

For the year Jan. 1–Dec. 31, 2010, or other tax year beginning , 2010, ending , 20 | OMB No. 1545-0074

Your first name and initial	Last name	**Your social security number**
If a joint return, spouse's first name and initial	Last name	**Spouse's social security number**
Home address (number and street). If you have a P.O. box, see instructions.	Apt. no.	▲ Make sure the SSN(s) above and on line 6c are correct.
City, town or post office, state, and ZIP code. If you have a foreign address, see instructions.		Checking a box below will not change your tax or refund.

Presidential Election Campaign ▶ Check here if you, or your spouse if filing jointly, want $3 to go to this fund . . . . . ▶ ☐ You ☐ Spouse

Filing Status

Check only one box.

1 ☐ Single
2 ☐ Married filing jointly (even if only one had income)
3 ☐ Married filing separately. Enter spouse's SSN above and full name here. ▶
4 ☐ Head of household (with qualifying person). (See instructions.) If the qualifying person is a child but not your dependent, enter this child's name here. ▶
5 ☐ Qualifying widow(er) with dependent child

Exemptions

6a ☐ **Yourself.** If someone can claim you as a dependent, **do not** check box 6a . . . . . .
b ☐ **Spouse** . . . .
c **Dependents:**

(1) First name Last name	(2) Dependent's social security number	(3) Dependent's relationship to you	(4) ✓ if child under age 17 qualifying for child tax credit (see page 15)
			☐
			☐
			☐
			☐

If more than four dependents, see instructions and check here ▶ ☐

d Total number of exemptions claimed . . . .

Boxes checked on 6a and 6b ____
No. of children on 6c who:
• lived with you ____
• did not live with you due to divorce or separation (see instructions) ____
Dependents on 6c not entered above ____
Add numbers on lines above ▶ ☐

Income

Attach Form(s) W-2 here. Also attach Forms W-2G and 1099-R if tax was withheld.

If you did not get a W-2, see page 20.

Enclose, but do not attach, any payment. Also, please use **Form 1040-V.**

7	Wages, salaries, tips, etc. Attach Form(s) W-2		7
8a	**Taxable** interest. Attach Schedule B if required		8a
b	**Tax-exempt** interest. **Do not** include on line 8a	8b	
9a	Ordinary dividends. Attach Schedule B if required		9a
b	Qualified dividends	9b	
10	Taxable refunds, credits, or offsets of state and local income taxes		10
11	Alimony received		11
12	Business income or (loss). Attach Schedule C or C-EZ		12
13	Capital gain or (loss). Attach Schedule D if required. If not required, check here ▶ ☐		13
14	Other gains or (losses). Attach Form 4797		14
15a	IRA distributions 15a	b Taxable amount	15b
16a	Pensions and annuities 16a	b Taxable amount	16b
17	Rental real estate, royalties, partnerships, S corporations, trusts, etc. Attach Schedule E		17
18	Farm income or (loss). Attach Schedule F		18
19	Unemployment compensation		19
20a	Social security benefits 20a	b Taxable amount	20b
21	Other income. List type and amount		21
22	Combine the amounts in the far right column for lines 7 through 21. This is your **total income** ▶		22

Adjusted Gross Income

23	Educator expenses	23	
24	Certain business expenses of reservists, performing artists, and fee-basis government officials. Attach Form 2106 or 2106-EZ	24	
25	Health savings account deduction. Attach Form 8889	25	
26	Moving expenses. Attach Form 3903	26	
27	One-half of self-employment tax. Attach Schedule SE	27	
28	Self-employed SEP, SIMPLE, and qualified plans	28	
29	Self-employed health insurance deduction	29	
30	Penalty on early withdrawal of savings	30	
31a	Alimony paid b Recipient's SSN ▶	31a	
32	IRA deduction	32	
33	Student loan interest deduction	33	
34	Tuition and fees. Attach Form 8917	34	
35	Domestic production activities deduction. Attach Form 8903	35	
36	Add lines 23 through 31a and 32 through 35		36
37	Subtract line 36 from line 22. This is your **adjusted gross income** ▶		37

For Disclosure, Privacy Act, and Paperwork Reduction Act Notice, see separate instructions. Cat. No. 11320B Form **1040** (2010)

Form 1040 (2010) Page 2

Tax and Credits

38	Amount from line 37 (adjusted gross income)		38
39a	Check if: ☐ **You** were born before January 2, 1946, ☐ Blind. ☐ **Spouse** was born before January 2, 1946, ☐ Blind. **Total boxes checked ▶ 39a** ☐		
b	If your spouse itemizes on a separate return or you were a dual-status alien, check here ▶ 39b ☐		
40	**Itemized deductions** (from Schedule A) **or** your **standard deduction** (see instructions)		40
41	Subtract line 40 from line 38		41
42	**Exemptions.** Multiply $3,650 by the number on line 6d		42
43	**Taxable income.** Subtract line 42 from line 41. If line 42 is more than line 41, enter -0-		43
44	**Tax** (see instructions). Check if any tax is from: **a** ☐ Form(s) 8814 **b** ☐ Form 4972		44
45	**Alternative minimum tax** (see instructions). Attach Form 6251		45
46	Add lines 44 and 45 ▶		46
47	Foreign tax credit. Attach Form 1116 if required	47	
48	Credit for child and dependent care expenses. Attach Form 2441	48	
49	Education credits from Form 8863, line 23	49	
50	Retirement savings contributions credit. Attach Form 8880	50	
51	Child tax credit (see instructions)	51	
52	Residential energy credits. Attach Form 5695	52	
53	Other credits from Form: **a** ☐ 3800 **b** ☐ 8801 **c** ☐	53	
54	Add lines 47 through 53. These are your **total credits**		54
55	Subtract line 54 from line 46. If line 54 is more than line 46, enter -0- ▶		55

Other Taxes

56	Self-employment tax. Attach Schedule SE		56
57	Unreported social security and Medicare tax from Form: **a** ☐ 4137 **b** ☐ 8919		57
58	Additional tax on IRAs, other qualified retirement plans, etc. Attach Form 5329 if required		58
59	**a** ☐ Form(s) W-2, box 9 **b** ☐ Schedule H **c** ☐ Form 5405, line 16		59
60	Add lines 55 through 59. This is your **total tax** ▶		60

Payments

If you have a qualifying child, attach Schedule EIC.

61	Federal income tax withheld from Forms W-2 and 1099	61	
62	2010 estimated tax payments and amount applied from 2009 return	62	
63	Making work pay credit. Attach Schedule M	63	
64a	**Earned income credit (EIC)**	64a	
b	Nontaxable combat pay election 64b		
65	Additional child tax credit. Attach Form 8812	65	
66	American opportunity credit from Form 8863, line 14	66	
67	First-time homebuyer credit from Form 5405, line 10	67	
68	Amount paid with request for extension to file	68	
69	Excess social security and tier 1 RRTA tax withheld	69	
70	Credit for federal tax on fuels. Attach Form 4136	70	
71	Credits from Form: **a** ☐ 2439 **b** ☐ 8839 **c** ☐ 8801 **d** ☐ 8885	71	
72	Add lines 61, 62, 63, 64a, and 65 through 71. These are your **total payments** ▶		72

Refund

Direct deposit? See instructions.

73	If line 72 is more than line 60, subtract line 60 from line 72. This is the amount you **overpaid**		73
74a	Amount of line 73 you want **refunded to you.** If Form 8888 is attached, check here ▶ ☐		74a
▶ b	Routing number ▶ c Type: ☐ Checking ☐ Savings		
▶ d	Account number		
75	Amount of line 73 you want **applied to your 2011 estimated tax** ▶	75	

Amount You Owe

76	**Amount you owe.** Subtract line 72 from line 60. For details on how to pay, see instructions ▶		76
77	Estimated tax penalty (see instructions)	77	

Third Party Designee

Do you want to allow another person to discuss this return with the IRS (see instructions)? ☐ **Yes.** Complete below. ☐ **No**

Designee's name ▶ Phone no. ▶ Personal identification number (PIN) ▶

Sign Here

Joint return? See page 12. Keep a copy for your records.

Under penalties of perjury, I declare that I have examined this return and accompanying schedules and statements, and to the best of my knowledge and belief, they are true, correct, and complete. Declaration of preparer (other than taxpayer) is based on all information of which preparer has any knowledge.

Your signature	Date	Your occupation	Daytime phone number
Spouse's signature. If a joint return, **both** must sign.	Date	Spouse's occupation	

Paid Preparer Use Only

Print/Type preparer's name	Preparer's signature	Date	Check ☐ if self-employed	PTIN
Firm's name ▶			Firm's EIN ▶	
Firm's address ▶			Phone no.	

Form **1040** (2010)

INDEX

HOW TO PAY LESS INCOME TAX

Step One - Learn What the IRS Expects

Annual Tax Mess Organizers are for self-employed people who want to learn what the IRS expects at tax time. It shows you how to organize a year's worth of income and expense records all at once, create a financial journal, and keep audit-proof records. The first book in this series will work for most industries; it uses explanations and examples that are broad-based and talks about a variety of professions. Industry-specific organizers contain only industry-based examples. For those who already prepare their own taxes, this book includes a chapter on how to fill out and file a Schedule C tax return. Choose the one right for your business.

Annual Tax Mess Organizer for ...

1. Self-Employed People & Independent Contractors
2. Writers, Artists, Self-Publishers & Craftspeople
3. Barbers, Hair Stylists & Salon Owners
4. Independent Building Trade Contractors
5. Nail Techs, Manicurists & Salon Owners
6. Massage Therapists, Estheticians & Spa Owners
7. Sales Consultants & Home Party Sales Reps

Step Two – Do it Right & Avoid Audits

30 Minutes to a Better Business: A Monthly Financial Organizer for the Self-Employed is a great second-year book for the independent contractor who wants to check the bottom line more often than once a year. It uses the same simple system taught in the Annual Tax Mess Organizers, and includes all of the forms you need to track income and expenses monthly, report inventory, and compile information that you need for the preparation of your annual tax return. Plus it teaches you how to use that information to improve your bottom line.

Do My Business Taxes Please; A Financial Organizer for Self-Employed Individuals and their Tax Preparers is perfect for people who use a tax professional. It will help you to get everything organized before your appointment. Forms for tracking business income, expenses, and other tax-wise details are included, plus there's an annual tax report section for totaling and presenting those figures to your tax preparer. This book uses the same simple method taught in the Annual Tax Mess Organizers.

13220115R00059

Made in the USA
San Bernardino, CA
13 July 2014